THE
INCONTINENT
CONTINENT

by Maurice Feldman .

Published by

**MELROSE
BOOKS**

An Imprint of Melrose Press Limited
St Thomas Place, Ely
Cambridgeshire
CB7 4GG, UK
www.melrosebooks.co.uk

FIRST EDITION

Cover by Spinach Design

ISBN 978-1-910792-07-0
EPUB 978-1-910792-42-1
MOBI 978-1-910792-43-8

Printed and bound in Great Britain by:
CMP (UK) Ltd, G3 The Fulcrum, Vantage Way
Poole, Dorset, BH12 4NU

CONTENTS

CHAPTER 1

***There are only two types of rule – good government
and oppressive regime. The former looks after its
citizens and the latter looks after itself.***

"Tomorrow is another day" is a common sentiment for those
weighed down with problems. As the day ends their thoughts
go to tomorrow when things may improve … hopefully …??

But in the early part of the twentieth first century, randomly
around the continent of Europe, many had come to the conclusion that their situation was so hopeless that there was no point
to tomorrow. To them, another day just meant more seemingly
insurmountable problems and so they tragically ended their
own lives.

One such incident occurred very publicly in the capital
city of Greece and the victim put forward some very trenchant
reasons as to the cause of such despair.

His name was Dimitris Christoulas who shot himself in
Syntagma Square, Athens on 4th April 2012. Mr. Christoulas
left a suicide note, a facsimile of which was released in its
original handwritten form by the Greek newspaper Proto
Thema. The English text is as follows –

> ***"The Tsolakoglou government has annihilated
> all traces of my survival which was based on a
> very dignified pension that I alone paid for 35
> years with no help from the state. And since
> my advanced age does not allow me a way of***

dynamically reacting (although if a fellow Greek were to grab a Kalashnikov, I would be right behind him), I see no other solution than this dignified end to my life so I don't see myself fishing through garbage cans for my sustenance. I believe that young people with no future will one day take up arms and hang the traitors of this country at Syntagma Square, just like the Italians did to Mussolini in 1945."

Dimitris Christoulas was a retired pharmacist and an elderly pensioner, so what drove such a person to not only take his own life but also to compose such a cryptic and graphically violent last message?

The economic circumstances which brought about his suicide were imposed by a Greek government at the behest of the European Union in order for Greece to remain in the Eurozone. Georgios Tsolakoglou was the first collaborationist Prime Minister during Germany's Second World War occupation of Greece. After Greece was liberated, Tsolakoglou was arrested, tried in 1945 and sentenced to death. This was ultimately commuted to life imprisonment.

Apparently in Mr. Christoulas's eyes the Greek government was just another puppet regime acting for a foreign power to the detriment of Greek citizens. And so he brands the compliant politicians *"traitors of this country"* whom he foresees will be hanged as a result of an armed uprising by *"young people with no hope"*.

The Independent Greek leader Panos Kanemos is reported to have suggested that the politicians and not "this man" should not have been the ones to commit suicide for allowing Greece to be crushed by *"this vice"*.

"This vice" has brought about many more Greek suicides. A 60 year old unemployed musician threw his 90 year old mother off the roof of a five-storey building before jumping to his death. On an internet message board he had written *"Powerful of this earth, for the economic crisis you created you need to be hanged. And that is not enough"*.

And not only in Greece. In Italy a 59 year old contractor of a family firm of two generations wrote *"Sorry, I cannot take it anymore"* before he shot himself in the head.

In Andalusia, Spain a mayor openly and very publicly looted supermarkets to feed the poor. *"There are people who don't have enough to eat. In the 21st century this is an absolute disgrace"* he told reporters.

The Irish Sunday Independent reported (September 2012) that in the west of Ireland the brother of a former Irish Government Minister *"walked to a derelict property that he owned and took his own life. He had become depressed in recent years ... once the bubble burst"*. A well respected local businessman observed *"Bad? It's worse than bad down here. It's a nightmare. My business is down 90% I haven't drawn a wage in years. My pension is gone. I've lost everything I've worked for. A lot of businesses around here are in the same state and there's nothing to get them out of the black hole they've found themselves in. The Government has ruined this country and they're not doing anything to give anyone any hope."*

Before the Eurozone crisis Greece had the lowest suicide rate in Europe but by 2011 this had skyrocketed by 40%. Suicides by men in Ireland during the same period rose 16% while in Italy the increase was 52% and in Portugal politicians blamed budget cuts for *"a thousand extra deaths"*. Eures, a

European Commission network estimated the daily suicide of at least one Spaniard due to *"economic precariousness."* Despair was causing a wide category of citizens, such as businessmen, the unemployed and those with low pensions to take their own lives.

It is not the fault of a government when casualties occur as a result of natural disasters. Yet the government of the affected country immediately makes strenuous efforts to alleviate the suffering of the casualties and usually implements preventative measures to try to minimise human and material damage in the event of similar occurrences in the future.

Presumably governments take these actions because to leave citizens unaided following catastrophes beyond their control is not considered acceptable in a civilised society. Certainly to leave the dead and injured to fend for themselves would be unthinkable – even in the most hard-line jurisdictions.

However economic disasters are unequivocally the fault of government and the casualties from the EU imposed restrictions are just as dead or disadvantaged. So what is being done to alleviate their suffering? The evidence would suggest that the life and wellbeing of the Euro has priority over that of the citizens and so austerity measures are the order of the day for however long it takes and irrespective of the misery and pain this may inflict.

The main bulwark of the Euro is Germany and it has to commit towards covering a default should a bailout to any country fail. Hence it requires very stringent budgetary controls by those countries to ensure that this doesn't happen. It is the effect of these which are causing the problems.

Although not the implementor of the austerity measures, Germany informs the EU of its conditions and the EU complies by imposing them on the countries requesting assistance through the various national governments. The differences are that Germany is merely setting out how much it is prepared to risk whereas to the EU and national administrators it not just about saving the Euro but also a lifeline to save their own skins. No ifs or buts – whatever it takes.

But *"whatever it takes"* is so severe and unrelenting that the term "suicide by economic crisis" had been coined. The damage that the policies were causing was no secret. Did any minister or politician ask – *"What are we doing? These policies are killing our people. Surely this is not what we were elected for?"*

They may have rationalised that suicide is not a typical reaction and therefore should not influence policy. When a Greek politician was asked on TV why no one does anything to help people who are driven to such extremes due to mounting debts, he called Mr. Christoulas a brave and sensitive man but denied that Greece's financial difficulties had anything to do with his suicide. He further surmised that he may have had debts of his own or even if his children had a hand in it?

If you visited your doctor and told him *"since I started taking that medicine you prescribed, the pain in my stomach has got much worse",* you would not expect the doctor to reply *"Poor you but there isn't any connection between my prescription and your increased pain. Perhaps you were punched in a fight or maybe your children tried to poison you."*

But that is because doctors function in an orderly environment.

In his suicide note Dimitris Christoulas specifically accused the government of annihilating *"all traces of my survival …"*. He graphically expressed his hopelessness and despair when the pension he had painstakingly built up over 35 years without state aid had evaporated and unable to rectify things at his present *"advanced age"* he had chosen to end his life rather than *"fishing through garbage cans for my sustenance..."*

Yes indeed distressing but the circumstances and intended consequence could not have been set out more clearly or simply. Yet the response to such a horrendous tragedy was to deny reality, divert the issue into the realms of obfuscation and finally throw in a red herring to make it look that the victim is the architect of his own misfortune.

Welcome to the perverted world of the politician.

Back in the real world, those countries with Euro difficulties have firstly experienced increased levels of unemployment followed by the ravaging of large swathes of their society as a direct result of policies to try to keep the currency afloat.

Irrespective of the reason for the difficulties, collapsing banks or bursting property bubbles, the result is the same – economic cutbacks, higher unemployment followed by unremitting misery for the unfortunate citizens.

The pain really started in 2009 when unemployment in the Eurozone countries known as PIIGS (Portugal, Ireland, Italy, Greece and Spain) dramatically increased, almost tripling by 2011/12 to over 24% in the case of Greece and Spain.

By comparison unemployment in Russia actually decreased to 5.4% while non-Eurozone U.K. rose to just 8%.

Suicides by economic crisis have increased as the economies have deteriorated and the increasing unemployment trends are the sure-fire indicator of nations in trouble. That means that growing numbers of desperate people in each country are just existing with their hopes diminishing as the jobless rates rise. Their plight was eloquently expressed by a Greek politician – *"death isn't just to die, it's also living in despair, with no hope."*

In so saying he appeared to have addressed one aspect of

Dimitris Christoulas's last message. But no one seemed to have meaningfully responded to his reference to the Tsolakoglou puppet government and his labelling the Greek government *"traitors of this country"*. To do so would have posed serious problems for Greek and all other Euro politicians for that matter.

Mr. Christoulas comprehended and had pinpointed the real problem. It isn't the Euro – he didn't mention it once. Occupied countries are forced to do the bidding of their conquerors and must ignore the impact of the pain and anguish this may cause to their own people.

He regarded his government as having discarded its obligations to the Greek nation in favour of obeisance to a foreign force and therefore no different than collaboration with an enemy of the state.

It follows that if the democratically elected Greek politicians are putting the demands of foreigners above those of their own local constituents and voters, then democracy itself has been gravely compromised. All member countries of the Euro are in a similar situation.

So the question arises – can any country in the European Union be called a democracy?

CHAPTER 2

Democracy is the means by which politicians can lawfully deprive citizens of their freedom

In a nutshell, democracy can be explained as the right of people to have a say in the making of decisions that affect their lives.

Does that apply to the citizens of Europe? The overwhelming number of openly anti-EU candidates they returned to the European Parliament in the 2014 MEP elections, would suggest an emphatic "NO!"

Democracy is a system of government by the whole population or all the eligible members of a state, typically through elected representatives.

Abraham Lincoln in his address at Gettysburg in 1863 said *"government of the people, by the people, for the people, shall not perish from the earth"*. This echoed earlier speakers, including Daniel Webster in 1830 *"… the people's government made for the people, made by the people and answerable to the people"* and Theodore Parker (1850) *"a democracy – that is, a government of all the people, by all the people, for all the people"*.

What is democracy supposed to do? The above quotes put it simply, repeatedly and emphatically – the people vote and those whom they elect act on their behalf, i.e. represent them in parliament. In a general election a so-called democratic country must apply the principle of "one man, one vote" allowing each eligible voter to ballot without pressure or hindrance. This is the *"of the people, by the people"* part but what about *"for the people?"*

Recent experience shows that as soon as the elections are over everything centres around the politicians and the citizens become irrelevant.

With virtually no physical or other connection to those who voted for them and certainly no indication of any obligation to try to fulfil the promises they made to get elected, a more realistic definition of today's administrations would be –

"government from the people, *for the politicians.*"

This wide chasm between voters and politicians has reduced an election to an end in itself and not what it is meant to be – a means to an end. Until the appropriate equilibrium is restored, democracy cannot be said to be working.

According to Robert Maynard Hutchins, the American educationalist the most likely causes of democracy's demise are *"apathy, indifference and undernourishment"*.

The "death of democracy" in Europe can be charted as follows:

1) Treaty of Rome	**1957**	*extension*	of European integration
2) Brussels Treaty	**1965**	*streamline*	the European institutions
3) Single European Act	**1986**	*reform* *more influence*	institutions/give Parliament
4) Maastricht Treaty	**1992**	*prepare* *introduce*	for monetary union/elements of a political union
5) Treaty of Amsterdam	**1997**	*reform*	EU institutions
6) Treaty of Nice	**2001**	*reform*	institutions
7) Treaty of Lisbon	**2007**	*more power*	for European Parliament

Each highlighted word denotes a lessening of autonomy for each member country and a power shift to Brussels. National leaders traipsed to Rome, Brussels, Luxembourg, Maastricht, Amsterdam, Nice and Lisbon and on each occasion, over a period of fifty years, signed away more and more of their country's freedom.

And so the lifeblood of democracy slowly seeped away.

While Brussels was methodically and ruthlessly appropriating power to itself local politicians were doing their own disappearing act at home. Over the years they had built ever growing barriers of advisors, bureaucracies, quangos and other stumbling blocks between themselves and the public.

As the law-making process shifted increasingly abroad (except for Belgians) the gap widened even further. In paying homage to their new masters, politicians diverted their focus to Brussels and away from their own constituents.

So who were they representing? Certainly not the people who voted for them.

This doesn't match the criteria for democracy so why are these countries still portrayed as being democratic?

"The Lord giveth and the Lord taketh away" (Job 1:21) but *"the EU taketh away and the EU keeps taking away"* (Treaties ad infinitum). One would think they know better than the Lord.

Events showed that they didn't because the public vented such displeasure at all this taketh away that the EU decided they had to giveth back something or risk derailment of their grandiose schemes. The Treaty of Lisbon was their instrument and true to form they still did a lot of taketh away by transferring even more power to the European Parliament and Commission.

But the giveth part was to grant a stronger voice for citizens through the Citizen's Initiative. Apparently one million citizens from a number of Member States have the possibility to call on the Commission to bring forward new policy proposals. However, it is not clear whether they can all call together or just one at a time.

Another was that sessions of the Council of Ministers were to be made public "in the name of transparency." Now this is really good news, especially for those states subjected to EU austerity measures, as they can now read all about the debates that led to the devastation of their countries.

Although these concessions were paltry in comparison to the power grab, it was enough to keep the opposition at bay by opening up more interminable debate.

Unfortunately, there is no scientific litmus test to prove or disprove democracy, at least by pedantic argument, but what about numbers?

"No taxation without representation" was part of a sermon by Jonathan Mayhew in 1750 in the colonies. These inhabitants were subject to laws and taxation passed in the British Parliament where they lacked representation and they considered this a clear violation of their rights. So deep was their grievance that it resulted in a full scale rebellion causing the British to quit the country.

It is known today as the United States of America.

In Europe there is plenty of taxation and very little representation. There are 751 MEPs and almost 400 million eligible voters which averages about 532,000 per MEP. The average representation of a Member of Parliament in the U.K. would be just over 68,000 constituents which is almost eight times less.

The 73 MEPs in the U.K. serve an electorate of 46 million (in 2011) which equates to 630,000 per MEP – putting each U.K. elector at a nearly 20% disadvantage over the EU average. But hold on to your hats for what comes next.

The website of a U.K. MEP stated that over nine million constituents would be represented by an MEP in the South of England. That equates to one person representing the equivalent of twice the population of Ireland!

Maybe nine million is an error but why bother wasting time and effort investigating? The overall European average of well over half a million per MEP is itself a preposterous amount of people for one person (picture ten major football stadia filled to capacity) and stretches the claim of representation to the point of absurdity.

In reality it doesn't matter because the evidence clearly show that the European Parliament and its functionaries have positioned themselves well out of the public's reach and exist solely to serve the whims and wellbeing of the politicians themselves. On paper, an MEP has been allocated to each elector, irrespective of how ludicrous the ratio, and this is all the EU needs to assert democratic legitimacy.

When a tinpot banana republic dictator claims that he is the legitimate leader because 99.9% of the population of his country voted for him, the EU is among the first to yell "foul!" But the electoral set ups in Europe are just as overwhelmingly biased to guarantee continuity for the pro-European ruling elite.

When it comes to faux democracy and showcase elections, the European Union can out-tinpot, out-banana and out-despot any third world country, so what's the difference?

The lack of representation caused by the preposterous MEP/ voter ratio, allows the imperious diktats which wreak so much havoc in the member states, to emanate at will from Brussels.

A scenario deliberately and painstakingly contrived by devious Eurocrats, embraced by the sycophantic national governments and inflicted on hapless citizens.

The "powers" (i.e. freedom to rule one's own country) that the politicians allowed to flow from their own nations to Brussels were in many cases won by people who were prepared to sacrifice their lives so that future generations could be independent and live in freedom. This hard won bequest was squandered as the genuine free trade area of the 1960's evolved into the grubby political entity of today.

To discard one's own freedom may be one's democratic right but it is questionable whether this extends to giving away that of others and certainly that of future generations. All around Europe, the resentment of growing pockets of disillusioned and dispossessed has been festering, both on the streets and through the ballot box. Increasing numbers are forcefully expressing their rage and opposition to EU involvement in their countries.

The EU is a system that requires politicians, especially those in the Commission, to give priority to Brussels over their fellow nationals and candidates for those positions are only too eager to comply.

The very existence of the EU depends on it being democratic, otherwise it is in breach of its own rules and cannot be part of itself. Innumerable tomes are written on subjects such as "Democratic Deficit" and "The Infinite Elasticity of Democracy" to identify linkages, however infinitesimal, to show that there is some connectivity between the EU and the citizens of Europe.

The definition that we take to mean democracy, was based on the model of a single nation state being governed by politicians of that state who were elected by their own citizens. It is plainly obvious that a government of politicians from twenty eight countries ruling twenty eight countries is not a like-for-like comparison.

The most ardent advocates of democracy acknowledge significant defects even in the single state system. How much more do these deficiencies mushroom in a multiple of twenty eight, each practising its own differing interpretation of the democratic process?

The EU model is a composite made up of two distinct elements. The predominant is unelected government by a small elite wielding absolute power. The other consists of politicians paying allegiance to rulers in a foreign land and imposing laws from that parliament on their own citizens.

Most notably, the principal part could not function without the collaboration of the leaders and politicians of the other entity.

There are recognised definitions for each single part and no matter how hard one tries to pummel and squeeze it, "democracy" is just not able to fit into either, nor indeed the whole. But should anyone say *"just a minute … isn't that the way Europe was governed in the early nineteen forties?"* the spin doctors and political scientists will be wheeled out yet again, to prove that even if it waddles like a duck, has feathers and quacks like a duck, it is not actually, a duck.

Not so Dimitris Christoulas. He swept aside all murky sophistry and equated the Greek government to a puppet regime serving a foreign master to the detriment of its own people.

As the Greek experience is also mirrored in other countries, was Mr. Christoulas not also delineating the factual juxtaposition of the EU and all its constituent members?

CHAPTER 3

"And now folks, to the continent that brought you The Crusades, Spanish Inquisition, Hundred Years War, Napoleonic Wars, World War One, World War Two, featuring the one and only Holocaust and the Kosovan Wars, goes the 2012 Nobel Peace Prize for its latest blockbusting bloodbath – The European Union!!"

Immediately following World War 2, large areas of Europe had been reduced to smithereens leaving millions of inhabitants in dire conditions. Construction and development were top priority and that was why the European Union was conceived – to rebuild Europe. As an afterthought, pressured by the USA, it was also thrust into the role of acting as a defence against the newly emerging Iron Curtain.

Europe rebuilt itself many decades ago and the Iron Curtain rusted away in 1989. Job done, so why does the EU still exist?

Because there is a third item on the agenda, still to be completed, namely the creation of a European Superstate.

This hidden timebomb was included (but not trumpeted) in the 1950 unveiling of the European Coal and Steel Community (ECSC) which was set up to reconstruct the devastated countries. Three years later France, Germany, Italy, Belgium, Netherlands and Luxembourg opened a Common Market for coal, steel, iron, ore and scrap inaugurating the ECSC which according to its founders was the first step to a full blown European Union.

However skewed towards politics the ECSC may have been, the devastated countries of Europe focused on its practical features to kickstart their economies as quickly as possible irrespective of the long term agendas. A starving man will not care whether his food has been provided by a burger bar or a Michelin starred restaurant – he just wants to eat. What was served up in the 1950's was an apt recipe and considering the pervading bleak and dispirited outlook at the time and who can blame them?

But now over sixty years on, at least two generations later and a world which bears no resemblance to the time of its founding, the EU politicians still remain slavishly yoked to the 1950's doctrine of dismantling the nation states in order to bring about a United States of Europe over which the elite political classes can be the supreme rulers.

Unifying or federalising the disparate states of Europe was the aim of despots and dictators like Julius Caesar, Emperor Charlemagne, Napoleon Bonaparte, Adolf Hitler and even Soviet Russia. But as history shows it was only a matter of time before their varying degrees of success ultimately turned to failure and the dominated countries returned to independence.

The EU does not employ armies to attain domination. Its modus operandi is the well documented, but immensely furtive, step by step approach. Six decades of a step here and a step there has embedded the federal ethos well into the bowels of the European Parliament as the November 2012 Budget debate showed.

The big debating issue was the effrontery of the contributor nations to try to keep the budget at its present level. One after another, MEPs stood up and complained that if the budget wasn't increased, there wouldn't be enough money for the sort of spending they had in mind.

The amount to which they were referring was 130 billion euros p.a. from which they take over 5 billion themselves in wages and expenses. It was puzzling how a sum of such mind boggling magnitude was not enough, but as some of their projects came to light, it became easier to understand.

Take the Stability Mechanism. Under this system, it was explained, nations such as Estonians and Slovaks contribute to pensions in other countries, although their own pensions might not be as high as those to whom they are giving their money.

What wasn't conveyed was that around fifteen billion euros up to 2013 and a further possible fourteen billion over the following six years, had been granted to Estonia and Slovakia by the EU. So perhaps Stability Mechanism really means giving away other peoples' money and pretending it came from those less fortunate than the recipients?

The previous week there had been widespread, co-ordinated protests, some of them violent riots, in 23 member states against austerity measures.

Their own budgetary problems at home and the sweeping scope of the civil unrest, caused many of the national governments to rein in their hitherto free spending ways and that included limiting the EU budget. But this did not sit well with the MEPs who seemed to take the spending restrictions as a personal insult.

An indignant MEP asked why the EU should have to cut back when it was the national governments who were responsible for the debts? In order to break away from having to rely on the member states for money, it was proposed that the EU must create its own income – its own resources were a necessity to fulfil the aim of a Federal Union.

But not all MEPs were singing the same song.

Mr. Nigel Farage MEP, U.K. Independence Party said the

British public was angry at the fleets of chauffeur driven cars, extravagant buildings and never ending travelling circus.

Fifty three million pounds per day, he went on, was the cost to the U.K. for membership of the EU for no benefit whatsoever.

Mr. Farage pressed on by proclaiming that in the outside world, none of the Commission and Parliament would get the cars, salary, pension or lifestyle that they get in the EU.

This must have been pretty hurtful to the chamber full of people whose sole purpose was to further the prosperity of Europe, but was it justified?

The debt per capita (the amount of government debt owed by each working citizen) in the Eurozone had grown from around twenty thousand euros in 2000 to almost forty thousand euros in 2011. In just over a decade the EU governments almost doubled the debt burden on their citizens until it became unsustainable.

Instead of prosperity, the EU delivered the worst austerity since World War 2 which is what it was set up to eradicate in the first place ... while the politicians themselves prospered.

Towards the end of the debate it was declared that compromise was the way to go forward ... "but not shoddy compromises".

In other parts of the world they reach for the stars – a philosophy of encouragement for individual effort and achievement. By aiming high and following their dreams, they produce such inspired enterprises as Amazon, Apple, Google, Microsoft, Samsung, Facebook etc. which effectively govern the lives of most of the world today.

Conversely the EU has to set its pace to allow the slowest, laziest and least talented to keep up and that is only possible with compromise.

In other words 'if we aim for the drains we are bound to get a bullseye every time'.

How shoddy is this?

The same clunky, bureaucratic, ante diluvian, megalomaniac ethos from the same clunky, bureaucratic, ante diluvian, megalomaniac politicians that have plagued the European continent for centuries.

As usual it is not the architects of the debacle who suffer, but the ordinary people on whom they inflict their hare-brained doctrines.

If asked what is so attractive about the European Union, the politicians answer "the economic benefits, of course" despite the facts painting a different picture. The only way to get out of this vicious downward spiral is for one or more countries to break ranks and run.

The closing speeches in the budget debate reduced the options to either staying in the EU and end up as a subsidiary backwater province governed by Brussels or leave and go it alone as an independent sovereign state setting its own standards.

In the U.K. the leaders just can't see it this way. They insist they want to stay in but only to avail of free trade. They are afraid that if the U.K. leaves the EU it will lose out on jobs and "world influence".

In January 2013 the U.K. Prime Minister Mr. David Cameron made a much heralded speech in which he declared that should he be re-elected in 2015 he would negotiate a new settlement with the EU to be put to an in-out referendum. He set out a number of categories such as Eurozone, regulation, power transfer, competitiveness etc. – aspects which constitute the core of the EU but which make the U.K. uncomfortable and which he wants addressed.

In putting forward that he didn't just want a better deal for Britain, but for Europe too he portrayed himself as the essence of tolerance and reason and to his gullible followers it seemed to tick all the boxes. But in practical terms it was merely an exercise in contradictions, illusion and futility.

The next day, M. E. Synon writing in The Spectator, a conservative magazine, reported that "*it is legally impossible for any EU institution or EU member state to hand back powers to Britain, even if they want to. Legal mechanisms for handing back powers ... do not exist.*"

It had been clearly stated in the European Parliament Debate that those viewing Europe as just a Single Market were fooling themselves and their citizens. The French Foreign Minister pointed out that there will be no "a la carte" Europe.

What's not to understand? But Mr. Cameron just stuck to his mantra that although the Europeans may want "*ever closer union*" this is not the British objective. Then he set out an a la carte menu with his choices to make the EU Britain-friendly.

Pure gold standard surrealism like deliberately getting on the wrong bus and trying to persuade the driver and passengers to go to your destination instead of the one written on the front of the bus.

It doesn't make sense. Why not just get off ... why get on in the first place?

In the Kafkaesque world of the European Union the characters find that the practical options are beyond their grasp – and that is the world to which politicians have led the citizens of Europe.

Meanwhile back on solid ground The Spectator's M. E. Synon comments that "ever closer" means that "powers run on a one-way street" – no going back. *"No EU institution is likely to advertise that fact to the British. The Eurocrats would rather let Cameron go on for years in what, in the end, can only be a pantomime of negotiation."*

It took just eight months for the playacting to commence. In September 2013 it was announced that David Cameron and Angela Merkel were considering cutting the number of European Commissioners from twenty eight to between six and twelve. What a crafty plan.

Fewer commissioners would not be able to run all the affairs of Europe so some powers could be returned nation states and Mr. Cameron could show that he kept his word to deliver a better deal for both Britain and Europe. The crafty bit was that cutting administration does not involve treaty changes and so avoids referenda in those countries where applicable.

It will be fan-fared as a significant UK gain but EU structure and aims are unaltered, so actually, no gain at all. Rearranging the deckchairs on a sinking ship may give the impression that the captain seems to have the situation under control but it doesn't alter the ship's fate. Presumably Mr. Cameron reckoned that such a manoeuvre should be enough to keep the eurosceptics quiet … and he is probably right.

What difference does it make whether a detrimental and unaffordable entity is run by either twenty-eight or just one person? It is still a detrimental and unaffordable entity.

In his speech Mr. Cameron stated *"we have the character of an island nation – independent, forthright, passionate in defence of our sovereignty"*. Britain, like all members of the European Union ceased to be a sovereign state when it gave precedence to laws made in Brussels over those from their own Parliament. Sovereignty is like being pregnant – you can't be a little bit.

This was painfully demonstrated some five weeks later when the EU capped bankers' bonuses – an action gravely affecting many institutions in Britain. This legislation was passed in a foreign land and the U.K. has no say in the matter because it ceded its sovereignty to Brussels years ago, so there is none for Mr. Cameron to defend.

In fact the U.K. had been vulnerable for years to Brussels-based laws but initially it was mostly about size of cabbages, shape of bananas – the type of things that are derided in the press but don't ring alarm bells. The self-serving politicians with their focus more on cosying up to Brussels than safe-guarding their own country's interests still didn't comprehend the havoc that can be wreaked by EU member states ganging up against Britain. What is worse is that most of them don't even care.

It just needs a majority to pass laws seriously detrimental to the U.K. and that is exactly what happened next.

The Prime Minister in "*forthright and passionate … defence of our sovereignty*" had "*real concerns about the proposals*" and sent his Chancellor to Brussels to block the new legislation but he was outvoted twenty six to one and that was that. The EU ministers decided to dig in their heels and simply not give way.

Not necessarily a sterling defence in the tradition of great British battles but probably the best that the feeble politicians of today could mount against some of the worst basket case economies in the world who now can determine the laws of the U.K.

What is the point of being paranoid about defending the country against terrorist attacks yet leave it wide open to wide-spread devastation by allowing foreigners to pass laws which strike at the heart of the nation's wellbeing?

In 1993 the IRA caused severe human and material damage when they blew up the City of London but the ability of the financial centre to function was relatively unimpaired. The EU bonus cap legislation had the potential to inflict incomparably more financial and economic harm on the U.K. than the whole of the IRA campaign, yet the IRA was classified as an enemy of the state but the EU as an essential ally and partner.

With friends like that who needs terrorists?

In stark contrast, Iceland is the exemplification of an island nation exercising "*forthright and passionate defence*" of its sovereignty. In June 2013 it withdrew its application to join the EU, but because of protocol that remains on the table for another four years pending a referendum – if they are bothered to have one.

Iceland, an island of almost 40,000 square miles, at the convergence of the North Atlantic and Arctic Oceans was economically devastated in 2008 by the failure of its banks and with a population of only 320,000 is the most sparsely populated country in Europe.

Having been forced to take an IMF bailout, two years of painful economic contraction followed. One couldn't dream up a more suitable candidate to be added to the EU's spider's web and surely the Euro-billions that would be dangled in front of them would be irresistible?

The EU wanted to impose strict quotas over its fishing but the Icelanders considered they knew more about fishing than the Union. In fact they reckoned they could teach Brussels a thing or two about fish and not the other way around.

They refused to relinquish sovereignty of their industry and sent the incredulous EU officials packing with their tails between their legs. The Eurobullies were obviously out of their depth negotiating with a nation with backbone, integrity and self-confidence as such characteristics are not the norm within their own domain.

Today Iceland can continue to fish unhindered and make its own rules for its own industries. On the other hand there is the ignominious spectacle of Britain with a population 190 times that of Iceland, having to go cap in hand to the European Court (September 2013) and begging obsequiously to whoever will listen in a vain attempt to regain lost independence over its financial sector.

Since that occasion there have been further representations to Brussels on financial and other issues, each determined by the level of clamour on whatever EU diktat was causing the British public most disgruntlement.

Somehow UK sovereignty seems pretty thin on the ground despite what Mr. Cameron says.

Another humiliation occurred in June 2014, when Jean-Claude Juncker, a politician from Luxembourg was appointed President of the European Commission. Mr. Juncker being in favour of a federal Europe was naturally opposed by the U.K. Prime Minister and when it came to a final vote, Mr. Cameron was outvoted by twenty six to two.

So much for the U.K. leaders' tiresome claims of the necessity to be in the EU in order to have a "strong voice" in Europe. This much vaunted exhortation was shown to be meaningless as the U.K. was annihilated once again in another "forthright and passionate defence of its sovereignty", but this time at Prime Ministerial level.

Mr. Cameron's strategy had been heavily criticised but as the other leaders were up for a federal superstate, he didn't have much of a chance.

A feature worth pondering is that Luxembourg has been a member of twice as many Customs Unions as any of the others, including Germany. It joined the original Zollverein (Customs Union) in 1842, left it in 1918, then melded to two other European countries, it hooked up with the present one at its inception, albeit with only one syllable of its name intact.

These contortions tend to show that joining Custom Unions is more a mainland European trait than that of an island nation. Neighbours living on each other's doorstep would naturally tend to be more adept and comfortable at getting into bed with one another than someone who is separated from them by water.

Also, the founding countries may probably prefer to have someone from a neighbouring country in charge as their proximity can make it easier to ensure that policies do not adversely affect their mutual interests.

This does not apply to island Britain, nor for that matter, the other more remote members who are pointedly not regarded as "family" by the joined-at-the-hip neighbours which form the core of the EU. So by what political wisdom have those leaders allowed their countries to be subjected to the authority of a politician over whom they have absolutely no clout and who is from a country with a total population which is less than that of many British and European towns?

An Italian described U.K. politicians as *"not made of the same stuff as Francis Drake and the other magnificent adventurers who created the Empire."*

How fitting a description. The concern is that it was Benito Mussolini who said it in 1940. No change in 75 years except today there is no Winston Churchill so the forecast is … outlook very gloomy.

The cold reality is that no EU state can call itself independent or free from external control, so what does that make politicians who insist that their nation remains members of European Union?

Collaborators and traitors was how Dimitris Christoulas

described those of his fellow countrymen who aided and abetted foreign powers exerting control over his country.

Message from current U.K. leaders to Francis Drake, Lord Nelson, Duke of Wellington and Winston Churchill –

"You needn't have bothered."

CHAPTER 4

"Let's have some fun. When I say ready steady go, release the Euro!!"

On 1st September 1939 Adolf Hitler let loose Blitzkrieg on Poland and it took almost a month to overcome the country. Some sixty years later, on 1st January 1999, Eurokrieg was launched and within just one day eleven countries had been subdued.

Different methods, different timescales but the same outcome – the subjugated countries had lost their sovereignty to a foreign power. The difference was that Poland had fought literally to the death to try to retain its independence whereas in 1999 eleven governments willingly volunteered to sell out their country's birthrights, not for the customary mess of potage but for a mess called the Single Currency otherwise known as the Euro.

A currency per se cannot wreak havoc – it merely functions in accordance with the features built in by its creators. So what is a currency supposed to do?

Abraham Lincoln during the American Civil War (1861–1865) said *"The government should create, issue and circulate all the currency and credit needed to satisfy the spending power of the government and the buying powers of the consumers … The privilege of creating money is not only the supreme prerogative of government but it is the government's greatest creative opportunity"*.

This was when the United States printed money without

silver or gold backing and declared it legal tender. Although needing currency mainly to fight the Civil War, from his description he seems actually excited that the newfound flexibility would beneficially serve not just the government but also its citizens who as consumers could enjoy the spending power it would afford them. President Lincoln is also very clear that the creation of money is *"the supreme prerogative of government"*.

Most countries took a similar approach and the accepted norm became ONE NATION, ONE CURRENCY. This meant that only single, sovereign governments regulated their own single sovereign currency.

That is, until the Eurocrats became impatient with the lack of movement towards their Holy Grail of a European super-state and decided to re-write the rules. Their first attempt was in 1970 when they commissioned the Werner Report. The European Coal and Steel Community had morphed into the EEC (European Economic Community) and Pierre Werner, Prime Minister of Luxembourg was appointed to head a group of experts to spur progress towards a common currency.

Mr. Werner managed to get all the member states on board and in 1971 the first of three stages was set in motion to achieve full blown Economic Monetary Union (EMU) over a period of ten years.

It soon ran into difficulties from external factors such as international currency instability, oil crises and other global financial shocks which culminated in its suspension. So the EEC just continued to run merrily along as a free trading area and had doubled its membership to twelve by 1988 when a new Euroarchy decided to have another attempt.

This time they took a more ruthless approach and appointed Jacques Delors, President of the Commission (and also one of the leading federalists) to chair an "ad hoc Committee" of the Central Bank Governors of the then twelve member states. The following year the Delors Report was presented to the public and just one year later, in 1990, yet another first stage commenced to introduce a single currency culminating in the launching of the Euro in 1999, all according to plan.

But alas, and not according to plan, in less than a decade it had pushed the world to the brink of economic disaster.

After recommendations from two such prominent politicians at the cutting edge of EU development, how could things have gone so wrong?

Jacques Delors is reported to have said that his report was a direct follow-on from the Werner Committee Report. So despite an interval of almost twenty years the two reports were similar. Not really a startling revelation – after all, each was concerned with the mechanics of setting up a currency … how many ways can there be?

The complication here was that with eleven countries, the principle of "one nation, one currency" could not apply so the big question is how did the two reports tackle the essential requirement of centralised decision making so that all the participants would be singing from the same hymn sheet?

The Werner Report is liberally peppered with unequivocal references to transference of power from the member states to a central authority.

e.g.: Page 13: *"transfer of powers to the Community level from the national centres of decision raises a certain number of political problems."*

        Page 14: *"it is essential there should be no misunderstanding in this matter, for economic and monetary unification is an irreversible process …"*

Page 24: *"and finally the transfer of responsibility from the national authorities to Community authorities".*

Page 26: *"the economic and monetary union thus appears as a leaven for the development of political union ..."*

Page 26: *"the centre of economic decision will be politically responsible to a European parliament."*

Source: Report to the Council and the Commission on the realisation by stages of economic and monetary union in the Community, "Werner Report", Luxembourg, 8.10.1970

It is very clear from these extracts that over forty years ago Werner had openly and unambiguously laid out that monetary union came at the cost of handing over national sovereignty to a central power. Furthermore the project should not start until this was accomplished and once in, there was no going back. This reflected what The Sunday Times stated in November 1970 *"a common currency is something that can only properly follow political union: it cannot precede it."*

If the Delors Report took the same line it is not apparent where these essential recommendations appear, if at all. They certainly don't strike a chord as in Werner,

e.g.: Page 10: *"the single market will reduce the room for independent policy manoeuvre ... it will, therefore, necessitate a more effective coordination of policy between separate national authorities"*

Page 12: *"indeed, economic and monetary union implies far more than the single market programme"*

Page 22: *"... a federative structure, since this would correspond best to the political diversity of the Community."*

Page 27: *"Discrete (sic) but evolutionary steps. The process of implementing economic and monetary union would have to be divided into a limited number of clearly defined stages."*

Page 37: *"The Treaty of Rome ... is insufficient, for the full realization of economic and monetary union ... a new political and legal basis would accordingly be needed ... political agreement would be required for each move to be implemented."*

Source: Report on economic and monetary union in the European Community, Jacques Delors Chairman, 17.4.1989

Ducking, weaving and allusions but no specific recommendations to political or fiscal union? Were they trying to lure the sucker countries by avoiding and or hiding the bitter medicine?

According to Dominic Lawson (Sunday Times May 2012) whose father Nigel Lawson had been U.K. Chancellor of Exchequer *"Delors, a highly intelligent man, understood the logic, but like the other Francophone architects of a European superstate, he knew the peoples of the would-be subsidiary territories would not vote for such a wholesale dissolution of national sovereignty."*

If this was the case it then follows that the creators were so hell bent on proceeding that they were willing do so at any cost – even to avoid openly and honestly tackling the vital requirement of each member state giving up control of its own monetary system.

And so the Euro was cynically and recklessly launched on a wing and a prayer rather than on solid economic principles.

Ambrose Evans-Pritchard International Business Editor of the *Daily Telegraph* wrote *"Jacques Delors and fellow fathers of EMU were told by Commission economists in the early 1990's that this reckless adventure would lead to a traumatic crisis. They shrugged off the warnings ... Mr. Delors told colleagues that any crisis would be a "beneficial crisis" allowing the EU to break down resistance to fiscal federalism and to accumulate fresh power."*

"Once the currency was in existence, EU states would have to give up national sovereignty to make it work ... Bring the crisis on."

We are talking here about deliberately creating conditions that will inevitably cause a crisis so that the participating countries will have to give up their sovereignty in order to save themselves and BINGO!! one European Superstate as ordered.

Ingenious, n'est pas? In the eyes of the leaders, the purpose of EMU was political, not economic so why bother listening to the economists? Only one drawback – what if they were unable to contain the upcoming crises?

That thought never even crossed their minds. As the inevitable crises occurred, in every case the country in trouble accepted whatever terms were put to it, just as predicted. That is until July 2015 when the Greek people said "No" and gave rise to the mother of all crises ... so far ...

However with its built-in propensity for crises, does it not follow that even if Greece had voted "Yes", the Euro would not have been any less prone to catastrophes cropping up for as long as it existed?

The structure of the Werner Report was designed around the six founder members of the ECSC (which became the Common Market) and in 1970, there were still only six. In 1989 at the time of the Delors Report there were twelve member states of which eleven had opted to join the Single Currency.

How can a structure originally designed to suit six closely

knit nations which together transformed a destitute continent into an economic powerhouse equally accommodate the inclusion of six further countries with no common connections and then another five later with more to come? At best it is suspect and at worst it is decrepit, even before it starts.

If Boeing or Airbus had designed an airplane to carry 100 passengers and later were told it would now need to carry three times that amount, they would inevitably go back to the drawing board. A completely new plane may have to be developed, because with the extra payload, the original prototype would probably have had a built-in predisposition to crash.

Any structure which is inherently defective will sooner or later need artificial struts to prevent it falling down. The timeframe to its inevitable total collapse simply depends on when such supports are no longer capable of keeping it standing, or when their availability runs out – whichever is the soonest.

If the fundamentals are not sound everything that follows is rotten.

The absence of any economic or indeed common sense to the motley and disparate bunch the EU was eager to pick for their Team Euro merely proved to further weaken the already compromised edifice.

No political union, at least eighteen having to squeeze into a system designed for six … but that wasn't the end of the bad news.

In 2011 to a request by the German weekly magazine, Spiegel, the German government published documents proving that Italy should never have been accepted into the common currency zone. The decision to include Italy was based on … *"political rather than economic considerations."*

In such manner all "distractions" were swept aside and the euro was born. *A sickly premature baby"* was how Gerhard

Schroeder described it.

Mr. Schroeder became Chancellor of Germany in 1998 but his predecessor, the formidable Helmut Kohl, who had master-minded the re-unification of Germany, had already forced through the common currency. *"I acted like a dictator to bring in the euro … I knew that I could never win a referendum in Germany … I would have lost and by seven to three"* admitted Mr. Kohl in 2002 to Jens Peter Paul, a journalist doing a PhD thesis. (*The Telegraph* April 2013)

In 1995 according to Bernard Connolly, former head of the European Commission's monetary affairs department, Mr. Kohl was being *"squeezed hard"* by France and the German political establishment on one side and the Bundesbank and the German public on the other. There were a number of issues, but the Bundesbank broadly sticking to empirical economic principles, wanted strict enforcement of strict rules for EMU whereas the other side wanted a more lax regime.

Mr. Connolly wrote that Mr. Kohl acceded to French President Jacques Chirac's "frantic pleadings."

Score FRANCE: 1 BUNDESBANK: 0 *Scorer: H. Kohl o.g.* *o.g. = own goal*

One problem was that if the economic requirements were to be strictly observed a number of the applicant states, especially the southern countries would have to be excluded, at least for the immediate future.

Quite a conundrum? Absolutely not … there is no choice but to run a currency according to the strictest standards otherwise it will fail, causing all those within its jurisdiction to suffer severe financial hardships.

But that rule applies only to currencies which are created

for reasons and purposes economic.

As has been well documented, the purpose of the euro was to force the European nations into a political union. Already many factors in its DNA had been based solely on political considerations, which meant that it was a political currency and the norms of economics did not apply.

As this was the first time for such a phenomenon there were no actual precedents so without further ado deals were made to get all eleven applicant countries up to the requirements to qualify for entry. Or more accurately, to reduce the requirement levels so that even the most feeble and unsuitable applicant country could qualify for entry.

In his 2002 interview he further said "*The euro is a synonym for Europe. Europe for the first time, has no more war.*" A pretty sweeping statement, especially if one considers that in those eurozone countries which got into trouble, the austerity measures resulted in people losing their businesses, their jobs, their homes and many lost their lives, albeit self-inflicted.

Are these not conditions that resemble war? Admittedly without the tanks, explosions and wrecked buildings but the rest is all there, including loss of life, loss of sovereignty and restrictions of freedom – not forgetting the severe financial hardships.

Prosperity would be expected to accompany "*no more war*" but it was mainly the politicians and the Eurocrats i.e. the "war mongers" themselves who prospered.

It would be difficult to find a more convincing example than Greece (one of the "southern" nations) to show the euro to be an unmitigated disaster. Yet in 2010 referring to the Greek bailout, the then 80 year old Mr. Kohl defended the euro as a "*guarantee for peace*".

Tell that to the victims (well … those who are still alive)

of his self-confessed dictatorial machinations the outcome of which blights so many lives in so many countries today. But Herr Kohl was not the only Eurogenarian who was in reflective mood.

In December 2011, eighty-six-year-old Jacques Delors denied that the problems were down to him. When Charles Moore interviewing him for The Daily Telegraph, asked *"whether he got it all wrong?"* he answered *"it is a fault of the execution, not of the architects."*

Is this guy for real?

As an "architect" he builds a house on quicksand and then blames the occupants for not living in it in such a way that it won't sink.

So much for The House That Jacques Built.

The Euro has caused chaos on an unprecedented scale yet Mr. Kohl and Mr. Delors were still convinced that what they did was for the greater good. In those days perhaps there was no one to tell them otherwise?

Actually that isn't true … remember Bernard Connolly, former senior official in the EU Commission? In 1995 he took leave of absence from his job and wrote a book which told the truth, the whole truth and nothing but the truth about EMU. It was called *The Rotten Heart of Europe* and he was dismissed for his efforts. His dismissal was upheld by the European Court of Justice which ruled that the European Union can lawfully suppress political criticism of its institutions and of its leading figures.

In 2013, Mark Carney became the governor of the Bank of England, but in 2008, as Governor of the Canadian Central Bank, he named Bernard Connolly as having been among the few who foresaw the global financial crisis.

The world at large should be frantically worried about the

Delors/Kohl successors who are just as infected with chronic self-deception and the mindless zeal to steamroll into existence any crackpot plan to suit the political expedient of the moment. Paul Krugman, Nobel Prize Economist reckoned that they worship cockroach ideas.

To control an outbreak of cockroaches it has to be eliminated at source. If only the European nations had the courage to take back the legislative powers to their own Parliaments, Brussels and its attendant paraphernalia would wither and die.

The predicament in which the Eurozone countries find themselves is a self-evident truth that courage is one quality not attributable to politicians. The skullduggery surrounding the EMU negotiations, although not in the headlines at the time, was certainly no secret and all the leaders must have been fully aware of the risks of involving their countries in such a botch job. After all, Prime Ministers are responsible for the integrity of their country's currency.

They had their own economic advisors who could have advised them on the prerequisites for a currency. If none of those books with the yellow covers, "Understanding Currencies for Dummies" was available, they could easily have just scribbled Abraham Lincoln's checklist on the back of a cigarette packet. For around 150 years, currencies had been based on this.

MR. LINCOLN'S HANDY TIPS for
CREATING a CURRENCY

CONDITION	DOES EURO FULFILL THIS?
1. ONE NATION, ONE CURRENCY	NO
2. CREATED BY NATIONAL GOVERNMENT	NO
3. SATISFY SPENDING POWER of GOVERNMENT	NO
4. SATISFY BUYING POWER of CONSUMERS	NO
MARKS OUT OF FOUR	ZERO
RESULT	FAIL

Compared to the robust Deutschmark which had kept Germany healthy for so long, such a wimp would be seriously vulnerable to any number of infections. Little wonder the Bundesbank opposed it. No doubt it also foresaw the trouble it would bring on Germany in the future.

Having been reported that the German public would have rejected such a project had they had a chance to vote on it, it is highly likely that the other countries would have done likewise. Therefore it is not unreasonable to surmise that all the Euroleaders were complicit in the conspiracy to create a European superstate behind the backs of their own people.

Furthermore, they introduced new legislation to regulate EMU, such as the Maastricht Treaty but apart from legalising the passage of the euro it also put more distance and more barriers between politicians and citizens.

As we now know, that part of the Treaty beneficial to the

politicians worked a treat but the EMU bit was catastrophic. According to Bernard Connolly, because of the "fudge" over standards to join EMU, Germany was the only country which didn't display the same level of enthusiasm as almost all the others. Such circumstances opened the door for countries that Mr. Connolly observed would make Mr. Tietmeyer (Bundesbank President) very unhappy to see included.

Eleven years later in 2008, Portugal, Ireland, Italy, Greece and Spain became known by the derogatory acronym "PIIGS" due to the instability of their economics as a result of government overspending.

Score MR. TIETMEYER: 5 MR. KOHL: 0 *Scorer H. Kohl o.g.* * x 5
*o.g.= own goal

The Treaty was sold to the public as a magnanimous gift of economic largesse from Brussels but of course the politicians knew exactly what it was really all about and made strenuous efforts to get it passed in the various parliaments throughout the member countries.

In those countries which required a referendum it was portrayed as Santa Claus coming to town and how the country would regress into Third World status if they didn't vote YES. Naturally the politicians deliberately hid from their people the real reasons behind EMU.

The laxity of regulation and absence of meaningful sanctions allowed the member states to indulge in the brand new Eurocraze, "Les Jeux de Profligacy Sans Frontieres." By 2008 Greece had profligated itself out of money and threw itself on the mercy of those who had written the rules which had got them into trouble in the first place. Soon afterwards other countries found themselves in similar circumstances.

The "artificial strut" to prevent the edifice collapsing became known as the now famous "bailout." The distressed nations, unable to raise money on their own accord, required third party countries to underwrite the loans in case of default. In other words thanks to the Euroflop, certain members of the EU were unable to raise funds without guarantors, just like children needing parents to guarantee bank loans because they are not credible credit risks.

Believe it or not *"… they're queuing up to join the euro."* *"It defies belief that Poland and others are still keen on joining the economic doomsday machine of the single currency"* according to the Telegraph's Jeremy Warner (March 2013) Another epithet Mr. Warner employed to describe the euro was *"economic death trap"* and evidence abounded to prove that this was not an exaggeration.

So why are countries clamouring to commit economic harakiri? From Mr. Warner *"… it's easy enough to see why the politicians are rather keener than the people they govern. As members of the euro, they get to sit at the high table with Angela Merkel and indulge in the make-believe of equal influence and partnership."*

What puerile behaviour, but there might be a different more simple explanation. Like maybe Europeans are just dimwits when it comes to economics and finance.

Wayne Swan, an Australian, was named Finance Minister (Treasurer) of the Year in 2011 by Euromoney, a prominent European financial magazine. No EU minister was considered good enough so one could assume that Antipodean standards must be seriously impressive.

Not according to Judith Sloan, Contributing Economics Editor of Weekend Australian newspaper, who in February

2013 referred to Mr. Swan under the headline *"Treasurer, But He's No Treasure"* placing him well down her list of Australian Treasurers over the last fifty years.

Not one incumbent from the EU was rated for the title of Finance Minister of the Year, yet the winner receives such disparaging headlines in his native land. With the bar set so low how appalling does that make standards within the EU?

Before EMU, if politicians wrecked their own country's economy the main fallout was limited to within those borders so in principle it was no one else's business. But because the euro is a collective entity, its value is reflected by the management of each of the constituent nation's economy so even the smallest hiccup causes ripples throughout the union.

These ripples have become tremors of earthquake proportions so how will it all end?

Imagine the Eurozone as a group of mountaineers all harnessed together on a steep mountain face. Many of them not only haven't a clue how to climb but also suffer from vertigo and if one falls all the others will be dragged down too. Even if some of them want to climb upwards or sideways, others find themselves unable to move so all have to remain hanging on grimly for life.

A snow storm has turned into a blizzard making conditions increasingly more treacherous and the climbers are desperately clinging on, afraid to move and unsure as to what the final outcome might be.

One scenario that can be ruled out is that unlike the movies, there is no Quentin Tarantino style rescue. In Euroland the only superhero is Germany and on that basis one can make an educated guess as to how things will play out.

So far German backing has saved a number of euro casualties but at the cost of severe austerity to the rescued and a diminution of its own resources. Eurofans will claim that there were other countries in the consortium, but this ignores the stark fact that no bailout went ahead unless and until Germany agreed the terms.

In the eyes of the lenders, Germany is not *IN* the euro – it *IS* the euro. When it comes to financial credibility the other countries are just not in the picture.

But there is a lot more at stake. Werner had stated in pre-euro times that EMU would be as *"leaven for the development of political union."* Although failure was never included in the formula, once it had commenced, the euro became an integral part of the European Union and if it didn't succeed there was the danger that could pull the EU down with it.

The extent to which Germany can stand guarantor depends not only on the scope of its resources but also on the continuing support of its electorate. Each guarantee makes the means to tackle future crises more difficult and at the same time increases the concerns of its citizens for their own welfare.

A measure of this sentiment can be gauged when as far back as 2010 Patrick Adenauer, grandson of Konrad Adenauer, Germany's first post-war chancellor, backed a court action to try to stop German taxpayers' being committed to EU bailouts. It was reported that Mr. Adenauer, a Cologne businessman, reflected the feelings of many ordinary Germans in saying that they don't want to pay the debts of Eurozone countries that got themselves into trouble.

He went as far as to declare that his grandfather, a realistic man, would have avoided this crisis by not doing what Helmut Kohl and Francois Mitterand had done in allowing unsuitable states to join the Euro.

In those Eurozone countries where money is being spent faster than it is coming in more bailouts will be required. But if there is a depletion of Germany's funding capability and/ or serious opposition from its citizens, eventually some future bailout will fail. When this occurs, will the distressed country be cut loose and left to fend for itself? Whatever the outcome, the eurocrats will re-circle and close up the remaining wagons to protect their own interests.

There will probably be a further rewriting of the rules, but the euro is already so malformed and misshapen who will notice?

They will spin the debacle as a great step forward in European co-operation and solidarity but the cold reality will be that unless Germany is willing to give unlimited and unstinting support ad infinitum, the euro will be deprived of its main artificial strut.

The early days of its decomposition brought ruination to countless thousands of hardworking citizens around Europe, graphically described by Dimitris Christoulas as having lost the means of his survival when the economy crashed and wiped out *"a very dignified pension that I alone paid 35 years with no help from the state."*

Apart from more grief for ordinary people, the latter stages will see the member states at each other's throats. This was well underway by March 2013 when demonstrations in Cyprus, carbon-copied Greece, Italy and Spain in blaming "German bullying" for the austere economic reforms.

"Support us, angry Germany tells the EU."

The Euroseeds were delivered in a packet with "Spendthrifica Mediterranica" clearly displayed on the label. Yet Germany along with all the other Eurozone countries couldn't wait to plant and cultivate them.

What did they expect to grow? Healthy, profuse crops of "Teutonicus Tightwad?"

What have the Germans got to be angry about? The scripture says *"as you sow so shall you reap"* and now they are simply reaping the harvest they had so lovingly planted.

Afflicted with similar congenital abnormalities, European Union was always destined to suffer the same fate as big brother Soviet.

The Euro merely served to accelerate its demise.

CHAPTER 5

"TO BE OR NOT TO BE" – to a politician that is the answer.

Adam and Eve were minding their own business enjoying the fruits of Paradise, when unannounced and uninvited, a complete stranger barged in and informed them that if they followed his suggestions their eyes would be opened and their living conditions much improved.

Subsequent events showed that he hadn't a clue what he was talking about and wasn't able to deliver on his promises. As a result they were thrown out of their home, their living conditions greatly deteriorated and were told that in future they would have to eat their daily bread *"by the sweat of your brow."*

This is the first record of a political campaign and although it is thought to have occurred almost six thousand years ago, nothing much has changed today. In order to get elected, politicians come up with ideas that are way beyond their capability to implement and the public suffers.

Wherever you go in the world you will see people of all nations working hard and on every citizen's back sits a politician using the sweat of that unfortunate individual's brow to obtain his own bread.

Because politicians are still clueless and incapable of delivering their promises, the worker has to toil harder and longer for that loaf from which the uninvited freeloader on his back takes more and more, leaving the unfortunate earner less and less for himself and his dependents.

O.K. it's easy to have a go at politicians but is such criticism valid or fair?

At the outset it should be understood that in no other profession can the actions of an individual influence and affect so many other lives. As such is it not reasonable to expect at least a modicum of competence by the holders of high office? But zero qualifications are perfectly acceptable and there are no penalties for messing up.

Accordingly is it any wonder that disasters occur time after time as a result of such unfit hands operating the complex levers of power?

Such an instance was when Gordon Brown, then Chancellor of the U.K. Exchequer sold approximately half of the country's gold reserves between 1999 and 2002 which turned out to be a very costly exercise for the U.K. taxpayer.

The issue was not the actual decision to sell, which is any government's entitlement, but the manner in which the exercise was carried out.

Firstly the mere pre-sale announcement drove down the price of gold to a twenty year low. Secondly the sale of such a large quantity over a relatively short period of time (395 tons of gold in 17 auctions over 33 months) kept the price depressed for the duration of the sales.

Suitable specialists could possibly have guided the decision makers through the intricacies and complexities of the commodity markets to obtain optimum return for taxpayers. Were such steps taken? Was there a rethink when early indications must have shown a disappointingly low price level?

In politics such questions have no relevance. With no sanctions when things go wrong, why bother going to the trouble to get things right?

Despite the botched sale Mr. Brown not only remained Chancellor for a further five years but in 2007 he became Prime Minister.

Politicians will argue that there is the sanction of being voted out of office but that is both simplistic and trite. Yes, they may be voted out of government, but they can still come back as Members of Parliament and there is always the possibility of returning to power.

More important, an election is no substitute for personal accountability. Rather it is a "get out of jail free" card for recklessness and gross incompetence.

This is not the way of other professions.

A surgeon who carries out a procedure beyond his qualifications and botches an operation to his patient's detriment would not be allowed to remain in his position let alone change to another field of medicine. Apart from the possibility of being sued by the patient's family he would most likely be struck off by his professional body meaning he could not practise medicine again.

Presumably this policy is driven by the concern that having perpetrated one mighty mess up, if allowed to continue, the next occasion might be even more disastrous.

Back in the political world this is exactly what happened. Despite boasting on a number of occasions "*no return to boom and bust … no return to Tory boom and bust … we will never return to the old boom and bust..*" , the bust at the end of Mr. Brown's government in 2010 made the gold debacle look like small change. It was so frightful that the departing Chief Treasury Secretary left a note to his successor saying *"I'm afraid there is no more money."*

With no sanctions or personal accountability, irrespective of the scale of the failure, many of those complicit in the wrecking of the U.K. economy were back in Parliament within weeks, pontificating and lecturing on economic strategies as if they had absolutely no responsibility in the shambles they had created.

And so it goes on … and on … in parliaments all over Europe … all over the world.

Each time a politician messes up more taxes are needed to cover the cost of the latest bungle and the burden on the citizen's back gets heavier.

In the face of spreading hardship, the ordinary taxpayer's ability to pay is becoming less reliable so the predatory governments in seeking new prey turned their focus on multi-nationals. Unlike the ordinary citizen who is as a tethered goat in the eyes of the voracious taxman the multi-national is an altogether different animal.

They are what it says on the label, companies which operate out of many countries. Each business function is located where the conditions for that activity affords most benefit. This includes channelling the bulk of their profits to those countries which are most tax friendly i.e. where the least amount of tax is payable.

Governments around the world are very peeved that they cannot get their hands on billions of dollars in tax from profits which in their perception had been generated by operations in their country. Among the highly peeved are politicians in the U.K. and in May 2013 Mr. Ed Miliband, leader of the Opposition warned executives at a Google conference in London that a future Labour government would take a *"far tougher unilateral line"* against the company if it continues to try to avoid U.K. corporation tax.

Google responded by saying that it complies with all the tax rules in the U.K.

If it is within the rules to avoid tax then what is the problem? Only that of the politicians' own making.

It was disclosed just a month after this attack on Google's perfectly legal activity that a supporter avoided a hefty tax bill by making his donation to Mr. Miliband's Labour Party in shares and not in cash. And another month later, in July 2013 it was announced that Labour had reduced its corporation tax bill despite being in surplus by offsetting expenses and tax losses from 2011.

Once again absolutely legal, but Mr. Miliband didn't announce that he would take a "far tougher unilateral line" against his own Labour Party if it continues to avoid U.K. tax. Why should politicians have to pay for their daily bread themselves when they can make others do it for them?

Mr. Miliband was a cabinet minister in the administration that left the Chief Treasury Secretary with no money, yet a mere 4 months later he was leader of the Labour opposition party throwing his weight around and making threats to companies which contribute vast sums of money to the U.K. economy.

It is estimated that British consumers spent about GBP £7 billion in 2012 on Apple gadgets alone. This would yield around GBP £1.5 billion in Value Added Tax and in other countries presumably the amount of Sales Tax would work out proportionately similar. Also, wherever they locate, multi-nationals provide jobs to sizable numbers of locals, pay full national and local taxes which contribute significantly to local and national exchequers – so why such ingratitude?

This stems not from a difference of opinion but a clash of philosophies.

The cumulative failures of successive governments in most countries have left the incoming regimes wallowing in ever increasing debt so they need huge dollops of cash just to stay afloat which in turn buys them enough time to make their own mark. This usually results in leaving the following administration with even larger liabilities. The phrase *"to pay your fair share of tax"* is trotted out but what that really means is *"we need whatever money we can get, however we get it, to stay afloat"*.

"Shareholder value", a term from the 1980's, is associated with growing the equity of the company and seems to be a major and aggressive focus of multinational executives. Critics tend to dismiss the concept as an excuse for intricate tax avoidance schemes. Maybe, but it also means making wise investments and generating a healthy return on capital to reward those who funded the operation. It is also a measure of the performance of those who run the companies.

Instead of hostility, politicians should perhaps take a leaf out of the multi-nationals' book? After all, taxpayers are investors in their own country so similarly would this not be a good yardstick to measure the exertions of their government? Obviously not by corporate criteria but say a simple appraisal as to whether citizens think they get a reasonable return from their Members of Parliament on their tax investment?

To start with the actual workers, i.e. Members of Parliament. Do they give good value in return for their wages?

In May 2013 discussions commenced to increase salaries of MPs in the U.K. by £10,000 to around GBP £75,000 per annum. An unnamed "senior MP" was reported to have said *"voters may not like it, but if you pay peanuts you get monkeys"*.

If the current level of pay is considered "peanuts" then that MP's pejorative description applies to the present workers including himself and his colleagues. Not a good beginning but never mind, maybe higher salaries would ensure better results?

The pay-scale of Members of the European Parliament

(MEPs) certainly fits that category. The following figures cover the term commencing July 2009 –

	EUROS per annum
SALARY:	**95,482**
ALLOWANCE OFFICE COSTS:	**51,588**
PARLIAMENTARY ASSISTANCE ALLOWANCE:	**254,508** (Max) *
PERSONAL TRAVEL ALLOWANCE:	**4,243**
TOTAL:	**405,821**

* *includes full time admin staff* PLUS

TRAVEL ALLOWANCE to European Parliament:

(For say a U.K. MEP can be approx)	**30,000** p.a.
PENSION SCHEME:	up to 70% in total
DAILY ATTENDANCE ALLOWANCE:	**304** per day

(Payment for simply coming to work, in addition to salary. Can come to very substantial amount)

The role of the MEP is to be involved in the process of making European laws so an MEP works in the European Parliament which "manufactures" legislation. That is then shipped to its customers, the 28 client nations. As shown above, an MEP gets paid eye-watering amounts of salary and expenses but to be fair, multi-national executives also get high salaries and expenses. Question is, do MEPs deliver shareholder value?

An assessment was forthcoming in May 2013 by one of its "customers" when U.K. Foreign Secretary, William Hague while on a visit to Germany, called for national parliaments to be given the right to show a "red card" to new EU laws.

"... ultimately it is the national governments and national parliaments that are accountable to our electorates."

One can imagine the panic that might have caused in corporate headquarters in Brussels.

"Quick, call the Sales Manager, we have a problem. One of our major customers is threatening not to use our products and encouraging others to do the same."

So what? They have to use our products, where else are they going to get their new legislation?"

"All our customers have their own machinery for making laws so they don't really need us. They never did."

"Then why bother coming to us in the first place?"

And therein lies the farce and irrelevance of the European Union.

It exists to produce laws for member countries, each of which already has its own independent legislature doing exactly the same thing. In the world of industry a product for which there is no justification because an identical item already exists, ceases to be produced and the factory is closed down.

The EU has a frontline workforce of over seven hundred MEPs, each costing over half a million euros per annum including pension. They are backed up by layers of administration and the whole packet totals around almost nine billion euros per annum.

With extravagant exercises of such pointless replication straddling so many countries in dire economic straits, one would have to conclude that in European politics, higher salaries do not result in better practitioners – just bigger and more expensive messes and certainly shareholder value deeply embedded in the negative zone.

The European Parliament would become obsolete if its lawmaking process were to be relegated to the decisions of national parliaments, as Mr. Hague suggested. The next logical step is surely to quit the EU and allow local politicians and citizens to at last regain control of the affairs of their own country and save precious billions in wasted contributions?

Such hopes were dashed when just a week later Mr. Hague's boss, Prime Minister David Cameron, declared that membership of the EU is in the national interest. This is also the view of the leaders of the main U.K. opposition parties and most mainstream political parties throughout Europe vis a vis their own countries.

Not all politicians relish this stance and Daniel Hannan, U.K. Conservative MEP wrote in the *Daily Mail* (May 2012) *"We thought we were joining a growing and prosperous market all those years ago when we signed up to Europe. In fact we were shackling ourselves to a corpse."*

All EU countries are collectively "shackled to a corpse" and none are immune from its contamination. Even mighty Germany who seemed to accept the fallout from Greece and another three PIIGS with equanimity, finally lost its cool with the fifth, Ireland, when recordings came to light of telephone conversations between managers of Anglo Irish Bank – the bank which went bust and bankrupted Ireland in its wake. On the tapes the bankers could be heard laughing and boasting at how easy they could wrangle billions of euros and making derogatory comments about Germany and German savers.

The German press was scathing, especially Frankfurter Allgemeine Zeitung. In an article entitled "Ein Marchen" (A Fairy Tale) in June 2013 Gerald Braunberger recommended that the bank's former executives be put in a big sack along with all the shareholders, creditors, members of the last Irish government and relevant members of the Irish Central Bank and Irish and European regulatory authorities. *"Then one hits the sack with a club until the screams of pain are unbearable".*

However the newspaper's prose, though melodramatic, does not even begin to address the problem. In practice it is as useless as a pedestrian shaking his fist and shouting curses at a motorist who has just driven at speed through a large puddle and drenched him. Unless he moves away from the puddle he leaves himself open to be drenched again and again. But he is shackled to a bunch of zombies who are unwilling to move and it was mere chance that it didn't happen before and there is nothing to stop it happening again.

Anyway why should the hangers-on bother when they know that they can sucker Germany into picking up the cleaning and any other bills? Was this not the essence of the bankers' recordings?

To add to the incongruity, at the time of these antics, Ireland was coming to the end of a six month Presidency of the European Union. So while the German press and indeed many German politicians were apoplectic over the irresponsibility and arrogance of Irish bankers and past Irish governments, the current Irish government was spending a reported sixty million euros for their stint as President and indeed hosts of the perpetually, revolving Eurofest.

Where did those millions come from if Ireland had to borrow just to stay afloat? Could it be that the Germans were being wined and dined on their own bailout money? That would be ironic – a genuine slapstick moment with Ireland squishing yet another cream cake into Germany's gullible face. How those bankrupt bankers must have laughed ...

How can it be in the national interest of a highly industrial-ised and efficient nation like Germany with over eighty million citizens to be shackled to the destiny of countries, some with single digit population, most without a significant industrial base and many with feeble and sickly economies and in hock way over their heads?

Perhaps Frankfurter Allgemeine Zeitung should urge the Germans to put their politicians and bureaucrats in a sack and do to them what they suggested for the naughty Irish Bankers.

Has the EU cast some sort of spell over politicians that makes it appear as a Fairy Godmother and prevents them from seeing the real Beast? This might be the case with the unelected Brussels hierarchy who never have to face reality but is hardly credible for national politicians who go home regularly and see the difficulties and in many cases the ruination of the lives of their constituents by the one size fits all policies of the EU. The mere mention of quitting seems to strike terror into their faint hearts.

They act like hostages as if they had little or no control over their fate. At the same time they are sympathetic and support-ive of those whom they perceive have imposed captivity on them and hostile to suggestions of being freed from their thrall. This would be classed as Stockholm Syndrome if not for the absence of one vital element – no country is the hostage or captive of the EU.

According to Article 50 of the Lisbon Treaty it is simplicity itself to break free.

"Any member State may decide to withdraw from the Union in accordance with its own constitutional requirements." *
*SOURCE: CONSOLIDATED TEXTS OF THE EU TREATIES AS AMENDED BY THE TREATY OF LISBON – CROWN COPYRIGHT 2008

Deep disillusion with the EU is no longer a prerogative of just the U.K. A poll of more than 32,000 citizens across Europe published in July 2013 showed that only 31% trusted the EU with 60% saying they do not. In Britain the level of distrust is

68% but that figure is surpassed by Spain, Greece and Cyprus.

This was not a survey by some anti-EU newspaper but one paid for by Brussels itself. These results reflect the shabby behaviour of national politicians who have stepped aside and allowed such pain and misery to be inflicted on their citizens by a remote elite in a foreign land – unless of course, you are Belgian.

It is merely another hard lesson (yet again) that Europe is not one homogenous province capable of being centrally ruled either by civilian government or military conquest. The status quo can only offer worse to come so surely the time is now opportune for countries to start packing up and departing?

Even with such overwhelming grassroots disillusionment no major political party in Europe is contemplating quitting. Today's politicians are not capable of independent thinking and the framework of the EU bureaucratic leviathan is to them the political equivalent of a dialysis machine or oxygen cylinder without which they seem to be unable to function.

Even U.K. leaders do not talk of actually leaving the EU. Popular refrains by pro-EU politicians and business leaders go along the lines that Britain is *"sleepwalking into leaving the EU"* which would leave it *"voiceless and powerless."* The very pro-European former Deputy Prime Minister Nick Clegg at one time berated his boss Mr. Cameron saying *"I believe in leadership … if you want to win the argument you've got to be in the argument"*.

Stirring words indeed but wholly unsubstantiated by facts. The U.K. was well in the argument as Mr. Clegg urged, in trying to protect the independence of its banking but not only did it not win but was routed at potentially great cost to the nation. The result demonstrated that the U.K. may just as well have been voiceless and powerless for all the good its voice and power did.

Contrast this with Germany who makes arguments disappear as if by magic so it can always win without even having to argue.

European Council President Herman Van Rompuy was supposed to prepare a strategy paper on the future of the EU and present it to a summit in June 2013. This didn't fit into the current thinking of German Chancellor Angela Merkel and Mr. Rompuy was cancelled in favour of a document written by Mrs. Merkel herself with French President Francois Hollande.

A masterclass in EU realpolitik that makes U.K. politicians look like wet behind the ears schoolchildren who just got a good spanking. Maybe it is this weak, weedy image that allows foreign powers the presumption to kick sand in its face by publicly instructing the U.K. on its EU policy.

"Stay at the heart of Europe, U.S. tells Britain" and *"America wants to see a strong British voice in the EU"* were the sort of headlines that appeared in the U.K. press in January 2013. To which Conservative MP Bernard Jenkin responded *"the Americans don't understand Europe".*

Mr. Jenkin is absolutely right because if Americans did understand they would have gone directly to the Bundestag, met the Chancellor and asked *"Frau Merkel, would it be O.K. by you for Britain to have a strong voice in Europe ... bitte??"*

Way back in the 1950's at the inception of the Union the U.S. publicly urged the U.K. to join so this sort of transatlantic undiplomatic behaviour is not surprising. But in July 2013 came a transpacific bolt from the blue. *"Japan warns UK not to leave Europe"* were the headlines this time. The essence was that hundreds of Japanese firms might review their position if Britain does not continue to play a "major role" in the EU.

The nub of the threat was for the U.K. to stay in the EU

so that Japanese companies can continue to avail of the free market – or else … which assumes that outside the EU, the U.K. will lose its free trade status.

At this point it should be pointed out that there is a world of difference in the terms "EU" and "Europe". As an integral part of the motley crew that makes up the EU, Britain is a mere patsy but as an individual nation on the continent of Europe it plays not just a major role but THE major role – possibly even greater than that of Germany.

Baroness Warsi, Senior Minister of State informed the House of Lords on 14th November 2012 *"My Lords, in 2011 the U.K.'s trade in goods with the EU was in deficit by around GBP £43 billion."* On the 21st May 2013, only eighteen months later, this had risen as Lord Vinson stated *"… the continuing £46 billion a year trade imbalance means that overall 4 million of its jobs rely on us? We are indeed its biggest customer."*

In the same debate Lord Tebbit asked *"… is there any other trading bloc in the world with which we have a similar size trading deficit, and which on top of that charges us money for the privilege of being part of it?* To which Lord Popat replied *"… there is no other country in the world with which we have such a huge trade deficit …"*

There is a further imbalance which does not seem to be included in the foregoing. *"Is my noble friend aware that our balance in food trade in 2011 was a deficit of £13.6 billion?"* asked the Duke of Montrose, presumably implying that "trade in goods" figures relate only to non-food items. All of which makes the U.K. a seriously heavy hitter and very much in the driving seat should it quit the EU.

Under Article 50 (Par 1) of the Lisbon Treaty any member may leave the European Union and from paragraph 2 of Article 50 *"… the Union shall negotiate and conclude an agreement*

with that State ... taking account of the framework for its future
relationship with the Union ..." *

*SOURCE: CONSOLIDATED TEXTS OF THE EU TREATIES AS
AMENDED BY THE TREATY OF LISBON – CROWN COPYRIGHT 2008

So it is perfectly reasonable for a newly liberated state to be a free trader with the EU.

Nonetheless let us assume that the Eurocrats want to make an example of the U.K. and tries to remove its free access to EU markets. Success or failure in such negotiations hinge on which player has the stronger hand.

This is an extract of the hand the U.K. holds.

COUNTRY	U.K. DEFICIT on TRADE for 2012
GERMANY	£19.8 billion (Sterling)
ITALY	£ 6.1 billion
NETHERLANDS	£ 6.0 billion
BELGIUM + LUXEMBOURG	£ 4.2 billion
POLAND	£ 3.9 billion
SWEDEN	£ 3.2 billion
DENMARK	£ 3.1 billion
SPAIN	£ 3.0 billion
CZECH REPUBLIC	£ 2.6 billion
FRANCE	£ 2.3 billion
HUNGARY	£ 1.5 billion

This does not include every EU country or those with which the U.K. trades at a surplus. The net trade deficit has been declared at around £46 billion (the above gross is around £56 billion). That is the excess amount that the U.K. spent trading with those countries.

With such massive buying power spread around so many members states, the U.K. should have no problem leaving the EU and obtaining whatever concessions it asks for.

In addition, from 1979 to 2010 the U.K. paid into the EU Budget a total of about GBP £228 billion and received back in benefits GBP £143 billion. The difference could be described as a GBP £85 billion donation to Brussels from the British people. By now that would be well over GBP £100 billion.

The numbers clearly show that the EU needs the U.K. far more than it needs the EU. Unfortunately U.K. political leaders do not understand these dynamics so they keep paying their annual membership (£12 billion net in 2012) for the privilege of being able to buy billions of pounds of goods from EU countries and being mocked and outvoted at EU meetings.

Even the most junior buyer in the smallest business understands the might of purchasing power but such a concept is way beyond the understanding of today's politicians. What other profession or industry would survive with such unqualified and unsuitable personnel filling its staff requirements?

Throughout the 1930's Winston Churchill ceaselessly warned of the danger of German rearmament and the certainty of war under Adolf Hitler. He did not come to these conclusions on a whim but by solid numeric data from reliable sources which he had set up on his own initiative. This showed astronomic German spending on armaments in blatant contravention of the Treaty of Versailles. Rather than make waves in Europe, the U.K. (with other European governments) chose to allow Hitler to proceed unhindered and for his trouble Mr. Churchill was treated as an outcast.

Familiar? Political establishment in denial; political

establishment marginalising Hitlersceptic Churchill; political establishment appeasing Europe; disaster befalls the nation.

The figures did not lie and indeed the pre-war government did not doubt them. It just considered it more pragmatic to make a pact with, rather than make a stand against … the devil.

In the early 1930's the amounts of German spending on armaments was not in itself proof that war would be a certainty. Winston Churchill's knowledge of history and experience of war led him to conclude that it was and he took every opportunity to make public his convictions. As a result he was isolated, pilloried and treated as a political pariah but he did not deviate. Ultimately when war did occur and a national government was formed Winston Churchill was the only candidate acceptable to all parties as leader because they realised that he was right all the time and was not afraid to say so.

By then they had allowed the country to drift into deadly danger and their backs were to the wall whereas had they heeded the figures and taken timely action they could have saved themselves a lot of heartache. Maybe even prevented a war.

The stance of the current so-called Eurosceptics is by no means comparable. Unlike the 1930's, today there is the luxury of a plethora of incontrovertible statistical evidence that the EU costs the U.K. significantly more than it receives either directly or indirectly. In spite of this, the Prime Minister and other establishment leaders insist that being a member is vital to Britain's interests and their opponents allow them a virtually free ride.

All the data clearly leads to a "get out" conclusion which is not the answer the political leaders want so they choose to ignore logic. They know that the EU will offer a flurry of token concessions which they will be able to dress up as a momentous victory. But it won't make any difference because the money pipeline from the U.K. into Brussels will remain intact. The sign on the tap will still read *"help yourself"* and the official post-negotiation verdict will be *"we got a great deal"*.

Even those who lean towards withdrawal come across as lukewarm and timid and keep referring to Switzerland and Norway as to how the UK might compare outside the EU. They whine about a load of rules and regulations to which these countries have to commit to get favoured treatment – as if the same circumstances would apply to the UK.

A fatal attitude and once again ignoring the arithmetic.

Norway has a population of five million and Switzerland almost eight million. Even the combined totals are not remotely comparable to Britain with more than sixty million. This huge buying potential makes it economically independent and actually better placed to get the EU to obey U.K. rules and regulations rather than the other way round.

Should the Eurocrats choose to make things difficult by threatening to remove free access to British products, the U.K. just has to hint that in response, barriers will be raised against EU goods. By return, it is likely that major corporations all around Europe will be screaming at the hierarchy to stop playing silly buggers lest they lose their biggest spending customer.

Germany, Italy and the Netherlands alone accounted for a £32 billion aggregate U.K. trade deficit in 2012, so without doubt the EU is the party that will suffer most.

Is it likely that all those companies which are warning Britain to *"stay in or else"* will re-locate their operations to countries that will become economic disasters without Britain as a customer? Is it likely that big business in these EU countries will allow their governments to play vanity politics in what is a very clear and straightforward economic life or death choice?

Even without the statistics, instinctive intelligence should pose the proposition *"surely we can't do any worse on our own?"*

But the mere thought of Britain acting independently seems to petrify the timorous politicians.

Take September 2013 when a Russian press attaché called Britain *"a small island no one listens to."* Presumably meant as a demeaning insult but still opened up a golden opportunity to show how well Britain had done in Europe.

Patrick Wintour writing in *The Guardian* reported that the Prime Minister responded by stating that Britain had *"helped clear the European continent of fascism during the Second World War ... helped to abolish slavery and had invented most of the things worth inventing – including every sport currently played around the world ..."* Later, Mr Cameron added references to the Beatles, Shakespeare, Elgar and One Direction.

Below is a summary of some of the impressive achievements –

ACHIEVEMENT	DATE
CLEARED EUROPE OF FASCISM	**1940s**
HELPED ABOLISH SLAVERY – most countries by	**1900**
SOCCER	**1800's**
TENNIS (Henry VIII real tennis)	**1500's**
STEAM ENGINE	**1700's**
BEATLES	**1960**
SHAKESPEARE	**1500's**
ELGAR	**1857**
—1973 BRITAIN JOINED THE EUROPEAN UNION—	
ONE DIRECTION	**2010**

Here was a terrific opportunity for Mr. Cameron to demonstrate the advantages of being in the EU and slam Euroscepticism out of the ground once and for all but all he could come up with was One Direction.

Brings to mind Orson Welles in the 1949 movie The Third Man asking what did Switzerland produce after five hundred years of neutrality and peace? The cuckoo clock!

Forty years in the EU and what did that produce? A singing group that came third on a TV talent competition.

And this is Mr. Cameron's *"key"* to Britain's future?

His list graphically illustrates the high degree of Britain's independence, standing and influence prior to EU membership and its abysmal decline following 1973. Today *"a small island that no one listens to"* is fair comment and in trying to defend the indefensible Mr. Cameron could only come up with examples which merely confirmed the Russian's allegation.

A professional unable to back up his public declarations with hard evidence would be discredited and find it difficult, if not impossible to continue to ply his trade. Not so with politicians who know they can get away with saying whatever they want, well aware that the worst that can happen is a few days of bad headlines. Joined up thinking is unnecessary, so why bother?

In August 2013, Money Advice Service, a government backed body found that an estimated 26 million people in the U.K. were *"living on the edge"* and 9 million more were struggling to manage their money compared to seven years previously.

Four decades of EU resulting in almost half the population living on the edge and further deterioration under way. The hard evidence shows that the small island no one listens to is suffering severely as a member of the EU so why do the political and business establishment continue to deny reality and persistently keep proclaiming that such conditions are in Britain's best interest.

Politicians have rigged the system to ensure that they don't suffer deprivation so it is in their own selfish interests to remain faithful to Brussels irrespective of reason or logic. Sense of duty doesn't even feature. European citizens cannot expect their concerns to be a high priority or even of passing interest with their local representatives unless it happens to coincide with EU policy.

If the living conditions of politicians were inextricably linked with that of their fellow citizens, members of parliament would then have to focus on the welfare of their own constituents who directly pay their wages. Foreign matters would be left to the Foreign Minister whose salary is specifically for that purpose.

The only way to bring this about is to get out of the EU. Politicians would not necessarily be any more capable but it would remove their protective barrier and they couldn't blame Brussels any more. This would make them directly answerable to their own people. Also it would redirect the billions of useless contributions to Europe into the home economy which would give some temporary respite to taxpayers until that too was ultimately wasted away.

Politicians restricted to acting within their own borders would be forced to live and work in close proximity to their own fellow countrymen.

Actually having to look them in the eye, they would be less inclined to allow hard working citizens like Dimitris Christoulas to be reduced to foreseeing their future as " ... *fishing through garbage cans for my sustenance.*"

CHAPTER 6

EU/USA CUSTOMS UNION
America comes to Europe – the Euro goes west.

A man walked into an exclusive tailor and asked to see a stylish jacket that was on sale. The tailor gave him the nearest to hand and the man tried it on.

"It's a bit short" said the man.

"If you squat down, that should make a difference" responded the pompous tailor.

"Wow," said the man squatting and looking at the mirror *"it's just the right length but unfortunately the sleeves are too long."*

"No problem," responded the tailor *"bend your arms behind your neck and that should take care of it".*

The man duly obliged and observing the result said *"perfect – I'll take it."*

He paid the exorbitant price and as he waddled out proudly wearing his new purchase, two nuns passed him on the street.

"My goodness, look at that poor man with such terrible arthritis" said one.

"Ah yes," said the other *"but see how nicely his jacket fits."*

And that sums up Free Trade in the European Union – cunning opportunists in privileged positions, exaggerating a simple concept to make it look complicated and themselves to be savvy in the eyes of a naive public by putting their gullible clients through elaborate but useless contortions in pursuit of their goal.

In that vein, a headline in eu2013.ie, the weekly newsletter during Ireland's EU Presidency announced *"Minister Bruton secures historic mandate to start EU-US trade talks"*.

The sub-heading read *"Potential for 400,000 jobs …"*

UK Prime Minister David Cameron said … *"an EU-US pact would turbocharge the transatlantic economy by delivering up to £10bn a year to the UK …"*

How do they know these things … where do they get those figures from?

According to Irwin Stelzer in the Sunday Times (August 2013) *"… informed guesses by economists, wishful thinking by free trade advocates and gossamer creations by politicians …"*

An ill-fitting jacket embellished with fantasy descriptions by silver tongued tricksters to try to make it appear suitable but invariably leaving the wearer excruciatingly uncomfortable and pretending it's the best thing that ever happened to him.

The truth is that anyone can buy perfectly acceptable and affordable clothes without having to go to a pretentious and expensive looking shop. Similarly, Free Trade agreements with the USA are very achievable without having to be a member of poncie Club Europe which constantly trumpets bog standard activities as stellar achievements.

In the hyperbole which accompanied the opening of discussions, one could perhaps be excused for believing that it was necessary to be in the EU but this ignores the experience of many countries, each much smaller than almost any European nation.

Like, for example, a little island in the Indian Ocean called Mauritius.

In January 2012, at a meeting between Mauritius and the United States, the Foreign Minister of Mauritius, referring to their Bilateral Investment Treaty said that they are confident that ensuing discussions can be *"a steppingstone towards the conclusion of a Free Trade Area with the US."*

So a country a quarter the size of the small island of Corsica or forty one times smaller than the much bigger island of Ireland, was able to achieve exactly the same goal but without all those puffed up overstatements and presumably also without spending so many millions of euros.

There are many examples of small nations concluding successful Free Trade agreements with the US such as –

Israel, including Palestinian Authority (1985)
Jordan (2001)
Singapore (2004)
Bahrain (2006)
Morocco (2006) to mention but a few.

The EU was only at the stage of talks about talks and this was nothing to be proud of especially in the light of all the foregoing done and dusted deals.

For politicians, lack of achievement is no reason not to crow so there is no shortage of hype which made some people very angry. In Ireland's Sunday Independent (December 2012) commenting on various clichés and buzzwords used by Irish politicians to try to justify the unjustifiable, Declan Lynch wrote *"They're good at that sort of thing, putting words together which seem to mean something progressive and uplifting, but in fact mean nothing at all."*

The article was entitled *"We've had enough of fat-cat gibberish".*

Stripping out the ballyhoo and fat-cat gibberish, what exactly is this proposed Transatlantic Trade and Investment

Partnership (TTIP) about? As a starting p
June 2013, referred to one of its "achieveme
Presidency as *"making it easier to do busin*

Anyone who is actually in business wou
used to be very easy, that is until politicians started interfering
and made it difficult.

Records show that countries were doing business with each
other thousands of years ago. It is even mentioned in the Bible
*"... a caravan of Ishmaelites was coming from Gilead, their
camels bearing spices, balsam and lotus – on their way down
to Egypt ..."* (Genesis Ch7).

The ancient Egyptians were masters of commerce and
traded their gold, papyrus, and grain for items not commonly
found in Egypt such as cedar wood (Lebanon); ebony and
ivory (Africa); incense, and oils.

If an Egyptian wanted some ebony or ivory, he would load
his camels with gold, linen or some locally produced item and
off he would go to Africa and return with produce common
to that locale. National boundaries were no impediment so
in the beginning trade was truly free ... from government
intervention.

As trading volumes grew, such a soft target as goods cross-
ing their borders was too juicy a revenue opportunity for politicians to ignore. So free trade succumbed to taxes and tariffs
which greatly swelled the national coffers but also became the
instruments to give domestic industry advantage over imports,
otherwise known as protectionism.

Each state or province set its own tariff rates and Europe
became a patchwork of individual economic fortresses making
trading a nightmare.

A momentous change occurred in 1834 when Prussia
and 17 other German states formed a Zollverein (customs

.ı) which established a free trade area throughout most Germany. They abolished all internal customs duties and enacted a uniform tariff barrier against non-members.

In 1899 a New York Publication, Cyclopaedia of Political Science, Political Economy and the History of the United States, wrote *"the economic consequences to Germany of the Zollverein were the consequences which may be expected from every custom-union."* It then lists – *"rapid development of industry … increasing customs receipts by increasing consumption … advantageous treaties with foreign countries …"* But most noticeably *"it increased the political importance of Germany, since its political union was destined, sooner or later, as it actually did, to spring from its customs-union."*

Quite remarkable. Over a hundred years ago, customs unions were hardly thick on the ground yet the Cyclopaedia of Political Science in its appraisal of the Zollverein was in fact also describing the features of today's European Union. But most perceptibly it put its finger on the certainty that in such an alliance, politics inevitably supersede economics.

Of course Cyclopaedia also had its own home country to study and few took to the road of protectionism more enthusiastically than the United States.

The same dynamics of politics controlling economic development was also clearly evident, so at the very outset the contradiction of governments controlling so-called free trade was well flagged.

Another model about the same time was the Corn Laws in Britain in 1804 when landowners who wanted to protect their profits prevailed upon the government to impose a duty on imported corn resulting in an increased price for bread and grain based products. Opposition was widespread and on those occasions when various amendments were debated, troops had to protect Parliament from angry crowds.

The after-effects of the Corn Laws' thirty eight years existence included –

a) U.K. goods became uncompetitive because higher food prices forced up domestic costs and wages
b) Unable to sell it grain, other countries deprived of income could not afford to buy U.K. manufactured products
c) Lack of demand for their produce pushed agricultural countries into industrialisation, creating more competition for U.K. manufacturers

The lesson being, that when governments meddle with the natural tendencies of trade it is usually at the behest of a special interest group. The advantages of such interference generally flow to that faction alone to the detriment of a much wider section of the population and is usually not in the best overall interests of the country.

Encyclopaedia Britannica defines Free Trade as *"policy by which a government does not discriminate against imports or interfere with exports."* Bringing together other descriptions, the general consensus is that Free Trade is international trade free from government interference which means importing and exporting without quotas, subsidies or protective tariffs.

No wriggle room there. Free trade equals no meddling by government.

Hardly an apt description of the Zollverein nor its successor the European Union. Both resulted from the conversion of a number of independent economic citadels each steeped in interference by its own government into one big economic fortress dominated by a central overblown administration whose sole purpose is interference and control.

A striking example occurred in June 1999. Europeans

travelling to any country even within Europe, used to be able to buy alcoholic drinks at duty free prices at the point of departure and on planes and ferries – a hugely popular and enthusiastically availed of facility.

This enjoyment was abolished by the European Commission because, according to a report in the New York Times (March 1999), it reasoned that if Americans were unable to purchase duty free goods when flying between US cities then the same restriction should apply to people flying between European capitals.

Instead of pointing out the obvious geographic fact that European capitals were actually in different countries, the docile governments of Europe went along with the Commission's demented reasoning and voted unanimously to abolish duty-free transactions within the European Union.

At significant discounts on high street retail prices this had been a terrific perk and injected a notable degree of joy into the drudge of travel for European citizens from all walks of life. One could not dream up a more heavy handed, mean spirited, punishing act of interference by government – the very antithesis of free trade.

Another gripe of the commission was that duty free got in the way of tax harmonisation but this pie in the sky reasoning caused even further distortions because much as the EU functionaries may hate it, the reality is that each country sets its own tax rates. Consequently after the abolition of duty free, some centres arose where trading became substantially more economically favourable than elsewhere.

Instead of delivering harmony it brought sizable price discrepancies in spirits and cigarettes around Europe, especially between Britain and its nearest neighbours.

Such differentials have resulted in a constant stream of U.K.

shoppers to France and Belgium to avail of the lower prices; a very undesirable and contradictory feature in a supposed single market.

This may be rather minor in the scale of the overall Union but it clearly shows the prime objective of the Eurocrats is domination and control over European countries and citizenry – certainly not free trade.

There are distortions and lack of tax harmonisation between states within the USA but it doesn't call itself a free trade area. It is a sovereign country and acts as it sees fit to encourage and protect its domestic industry. When the USA is asked whether it wants to discuss a free trade agreement with the EU, it can simply answer yes, no or maybe as the mood takes it.

In the case of a proposed EU-USA free trade agreement it was delighted to agree to talks especially for the benefits that would flow to US business interests.

According to Max Keiser, former stockbroker and creator of virtual securities, and host of the Keiser Report on RT, the Russian English language news channel, this "nod to business interests" translates as *"The US and EU's Trans-Atlantic Free Trade Agreement (TAFTA) aims to hand foreign corporations ways to evade domestic laws and courts while giving them the ability to sue the countries for compensatory damages from the economies that they've just devastated... it gives all the power to the entities that have destroyed the European economy ..."*

Under this scenario, the agreement would allow the US to jockey its large corporations into dominant and predatory positions within Europe and as an added bonus reports from the US welcome it as an opportunity to exert more influence over foreign defence budgets.

The American motives certainly do not fit the definition of Free Trade but what about the European side?

The European Union is made up of nearly thirty different countries, each with its own opinions. Experience shows that the smaller countries usually take the line that it is in their best interests to go along with whatever the larger countries decide.

The U.K. was all in favour, which is rather strange because the USA is one of the few countries with which it runs a substantially positive trade balance.

U.K. companies racked up an eleven billion pounds sterling surplus in 2012.

In June 2013 Mr. Cameron said that Britain must be *"unashamedly bold and hard-headed about pursuing our national interest abroad, rather than supinely going with the flow of multilateral opinion."* As the custodian of U.K. national interests this is the Prime Minister's job, but his support for the TTIP is in effect saying *"let's give our European competitors a helping hand to sell into America".*

Surely providing a magic carpet for foreign firms to gain access to a lucrative overseas market to compete against his own British companies is the opposite of "bold and hard-headed" and can only damage the very interests he is duty bound to protect.

How bonkers is that?

France's response to talks with the US was also an immediate "yes" … sprinkled with a few immediate "noes." Categorised as the "cultural exception", including audio-visual services which President Hollande wanted excluded from the negotiations.

Adding to France's exemption list (which by extension also has to be that of the EU) were food safety standards.

A big package of exclusions demanded by France, but wait … there's more!

The French also said that they were not going to negotiate

on the issue of GMO either.

About a quarter of all crops grown in the United States comes under the category of Genetically Modified Organisms (GMO) – food products which have been genetically engineered, so the discussions on food and agriculture would have been fun, but we will never know because France won't allow it to be discussed … well that was until June 2014.

Apparently because of American pressure, the European Union caved in and decided to allow member countries to make their own decisions. Presumably France can still refuse to discuss the matter but this won't affect the US from negotiating GMOs individually with any consenting states. How non-Single Market is that?

At at least the Germans can be relied upon for cool, objective judgement … that is … until they discovered that the Americans were spying on Mrs. Merkel's mobile phone.

Shock! Horror!! Outrage!!!

Mrs. Merkel was melodramatically struck down with all three manifestations and warned that the trade talks could be hurt. The indignation spread like wildfire, prompting many to go public with their "expert" knowledge on electronic snooping. Step forward Ms. Viviane Reding, a politician from Luxembourg who said *"Friends and partners do not spy on each other."* Ms. Reding is the EU Justice Minister so she should know … shouldn't she?

Not if we are to believe Bernard Squarcini, head of intelligence under Nicolas Sarkosy, the former French President. who said *" All countries, even allies … are spying on each other"*. Or Anthony Glees, director of the Centre for Security and Intelligence Studies at Buckingham University (U.K.) who said that Mrs. Merkel was *"completely idiotic if she did not suspect the NSA might try to eavesdrop on her conversations"*.

(Sunday Times Oct. 2013) Or most telling, that the BND, the German equivalent of MI6, monitored telephone calls as well as text messages and emails in the United States. The BND told German newspaper Bild *"we take what we can get ..."*

NOTE: **While this was playing out, reports published almost a year later in August 2014, claimed that Germany had been spying on Turkey, a fellow NATO partner, for five years and intercepting telephone calls from successive U.S. Secretaries of State Hillary Clinton and John Kerry. As America did not seem to be aware of this at the time, Germany was able to milk the situation for all the sympathy and concessions that might be going.** NOW READ ON ...

European Voice (October 2013) wrote that a number of German politicians, including Martin Schultz, the President of the European Parliament, wanted the EU/US free trade talks suspended because of the phone tapping.

Max Keiser isn't impressed. *"She said I don't want the NSA spying on me. Now she's laying down supine, just letting this new law which favours American corporations to roll over her ... like Bambi in the woods, just rolled over. She should stand up for her citizens."*

So the European Prime Ministers all lie down beside Mrs. Merkel to await the American juggernaut to roll over them. Although this is certainly not standing up for their citizens, they are sure of one thing – this agreement will be good for ... themselves and will put even more distance and barriers between politicians and the electorate.

And rolling over is not the only activity at which European leaders are adept.

On 12th October 2013, The Times headlined *"Britain and*

Germany in secret pact to defy EU laws … Britain is nego-tiating a secret deal to help to shield Germany's luxury car industry from new European rules in return for support for UK bankers."

According to EUReferendum.com this "horse trading" goes on all the time *"… and almost always out of the public gaze, with no records kept … that is one of the reasons why governments actually like the EU. They can do their wheeling and dealing in the anonymity of the bars and restaurants of Brussels … and then blame the anonymous "eurocrats" for the outcomes."*

In this specific case, German luxury car manufacturers and British bankers had apparently pressured their respective governments to subvert certain European laws which had become burdensome to them. And apparently this sort of thing happens … all the time.

In public, the wondrous benefits of the EU are extolled but the one-size-fits-all system of laws will inevitably have an adverse effect on each and every member country at some time or other. In order to conceal and minimise the inescap-able damage when it is their own country's turn to be harmed, politicians have to do deals in secret so as not to reveal to their constituents that the EU is not so wondrous and beneficial after all.

Like children being given runny porridge and soggy toast for breakfast every morning and being told by their parents how lucky they are to have such superb fare. Then as soon as the children have gone to school the parents treat themselves to a full English fry-up.

The overriding topic in the EU-US talks for trying to create the "world's largest trading bloc", is not Free Trade but rather secrecy – on an astounding scale, as a letter dated 5th July

2013 reveals.

This letter, on European Commission notepaper, is from the Chief EU negotiator for TTIP to the Chief US negotiator for TTIP and consists of nine paragraphs, each one referring to methods and procedures for keeping the negotiations secret and out of the public domain.

The EU Chief negotiator acknowledges the EU regulation regarding public access to European Parliament (Par 2) but points out that Article 4 of that regulation allows for certain exceptions ... *"for the protection of public interest ..."* so the only thing the public is allowed to know is that there is a letter declaring that other than the letter itself, everything else ... is a secret!

The European Commission claims that confidentiality in trade negotiations is *"entirely normal."*

Corporate Europe Observatory, a website aimed at *"Exposing the power of corporate lobbying in the EU"* says secrecy is not *"entirely normal"* in other international trade negotiations. For example, the World Trade Organisation members, including the EU, publish their negotiating positions. Also in global climate negotiations where parties, again including the EU, *"do not seem to see opacity as a precondition for a successful agreement."*

Even former US trade negotiator and president of the World Bank 2007 to 2012, Robert Zoellick, said draft trade texts were seen by hundreds of people anyway – government officials, advisors and lobbyists *"so why not simply put the information online?"*

According to Corporate Europe Observatory the reason why the Commission wants it kept secret *"... is about securing the best deal possible for big businesses, not European or US people."*

The stage is being set for "world's largest bloc of trading secrets". It follows that like any idea emanating from Brussels it will be great for the bureaucrats, politicians and big industry but as always, very detrimental to the ordinary citizen.

According to Max Keiser, *"closed-door talks for the agreement will ultimately create an "investor state"* system in which regulatory structures on both sides of the Atlantic are weakened for the profit seeking motives of mainly American corporate entities."*

* (investor or corporate state – where corporations have the ability to override sovereignty)

Naturally in the Commission's eyes it makes perfect sense to keep negotiations for the proposed EU-US trade deal *"… hidden from the public because if people understood its potential impacts, this could lead to widespread opposition to the negotiations."* (Corporate Europe Observatory)

Yet despite Europe stirring up all this cloak and dagger, on learning that the Americans were snooping on her mobile phone calls, a furious Angela Merkel is reported to have said to President Obama *"This is like the Stasi".*

Talk about taking a sledgehammer …

In East Germany, where she grew up, the Stasi was the secret police which spied on the population, mainly pressurising ordinary citizens to inform on neighbours and family. It was one of the most hated and feared institutions in the communist state and the information they obtained from their "spies" often led to the execution of those who had strayed from the party line.

Hardly comparable but was the comment deliberately exaggerated to try to gain the moral high ground? Like when others yell "nazi" to actions which may indeed be distasteful but are not even on the same planet as those carried out by the National Socialist regime.

Excessive and on most occasions way over the top, although in the case of Lampedusa, at the southernmost part of Italy, comparison with the Nazi era is possibly justified.

This little island was thrust into the limelight in October 2013, when headlines around the world proclaimed that Jose Manuel Barroso (EC President) and Enrico Letta (Italian PM) were jeered and barracked by the islanders while on a joint visit to Lampedusa. Up to 350 African asylum seekers had just been killed when their boat caught fire and sank in the vicinity.

"Fortress Europe responsible for deaths in Lampedusa" reported maltatoday.com.mt a Maltese online news portal (7/10/2013) while in Lampedusa hundreds of African migrants and human rights activists demonstrated outside the law courts carrying posters which read *"No more deaths at Borders"* and *"No to fortress Europe".*

Fortress Europe ... what on earth is that?

In January 2005 an item appeared on the World Socialist Web Site(wsws.org), entitled "European Union continues to build a "fortress Europe".

"The governments in Warsaw (Poland), Budapest (Hungary), Ljubljana (Slovenia) and Bratislava (Slovakia),Tallinn (Estonia), Riga (Latvia) and Vilnius (Lithuania) are charged with defending the new frontiers of the European Union to the east. In the Mediterranean, Valetta (Malta) is now the front line of defence against those seeking to come to the EU from Africa."

To get the full picture, think World War 2 ... think Nazi ... think Festung Europa which translates into Fortress Europe as the areas of Nazi occupied Continental Europe were known. Within this defensive perimeter was the Atlantic Wall forming a major part of Adolf Hitler's Fortress Europe. Its construction in France was by forced French labour as part of an arrangement between the Germans and the collaborationist Vichy Government.

Following a tragedy of such proportions within Italian territory, the visit by its Prime Minister to Lampedusa was to be expected but the presence of the Portuguese EC President who accompanied him, evokes memories of the iconic photos of Field Marshal Rommel inspecting the Atlantic Wall against an Allied invasion – a foreigner (German) overseeing the defence of French soil.

And some seventy years later the collaborationist nightmare returns, except this time on Italian soil. In his article in the Sunday Times Magazine (8/12/13) entitled *"Welcome to Death Island"* AA Gill spoke to the mayor of Lampedusa, Mayor Guisi Nicolini and she told him *"This is not a new crisis … we have been taking in refugees every week for 15 years."*

According to wsws.org a meeting of 25 EU ministers in Luxembourg towards the end of 2004, agreed further measures for strengthening Fortress Europe. These are contained in the subsequent Hague Convention, the bottom line being that it is up to *"the wealthier nations of west and north Europe … to repel so-called "illegal immigrants."*

How Brussels is that? Refugees have certain entitlements but change the definition to "illegal immigrants" and their rights go out the window.

Under the Italian Bossi-Fini legislation, introduced by a Berlusconi administration, it was a punishable offence to aid illegal immigrants, which put fishermen involved in a rescue at the risk of having their boats confiscated plus a hefty fine. How collaborationist is that? How Nazi is that?

But how is all this relevant to the proposed EU-US Trade Agreement?

A study entitled "Dimensions and Effects of a Transatlantic Free Trade Agreement Between the EU and US" dated February 2013, was undertaken by Leibniz-Institut fur Wirtchaftsforschung and der Universitat Munchen. It was commissioned by the German Federal Ministry of Economics and Technology.

The report is eleven pages, goes into fairly complex detail including graphs and statistics and its conclusion is generally upbeat about Germany's prospects. However four lines on the final page starkly state *"The central point of criticism on a comprehensive agreement between the EU and U.S., is that such a trade deal would put third countries at a disadvantage."*

For heaven's sake! These are the countries the refugees come from and if you haven't yet noticed, they are already at a big disadvantage. So if this expert report claims that an EU-US Free Trade agreement would be even more detrimental, could it be that the EU itself is putting these countries in trouble in the first place?

"EU subsidies deny Africa's farmers of their livelihood" headlined The Independent (May 2006) in an article by Maxine Frith. She reported that *"British households pay an extra £832 a year in grocery bills due to the EU subsidy system that is also depriving tens of thousands of African farmers of their livelihood....."* The Common Agricultural Policy (CAP) *"lavishes subsidies on the UK's wealthiest farmers and biggest landowners at the expense of millions of farmers in the developing world."*

"In addition, European countries dump thousands of tons of subsidised exports in Africa every year so that local producers cannot even compete on a level playing field in their own land."

A further example from George Monbiot (*The Guardian*

Sept 2008) referring to Felicity Lawrence's book *Eat Your Heart Out* "… *in 1994 Senegal was forced to remove its trade taxes. This allowed the EU to dump subsidised tomatoes and chicken on its markets, putting its farmers out of business. They moved into fishing at about the same time as the European super-trawlers arrived and were wiped out again. So fishing boats were instead deployed to carry economic migrants out of Senegal. Lawrence discovered that those who survive the voyage to Europe are being employed in near-slavery by … the subsidised tomato industry.*"

It is estimated that during the past twenty years in trying to seek a better life in Europe, 17,000 to 20,000 have died trying to cross the Mediterranean on overcrowded fishing boats or rubber dinghies.

On his visit to Lampedusa Mr Barosso is reported to have said *"that image of hundreds of coffins will never get out of my mind"* and was moved enough to announce an extra thirty million euro *"of EU funding to help Italian communities such as Lampedusa deal with the migration crisis …"*

Hold on a moment …

The Common Agricultural Policy deprives Africans of their livelihood in their own countries so they try to make a living in Europe. Then the EU has to fund the consequences of "the migration crisis" … which was created in the first place by … the Common Agricultural Policy???

A vicious circle to which there is just no sense – so what is the point of the CAP?

We won't get a credible answer because as the most costly scheme in the EU, (over 57 billion euros in 2013) the next question would have to be "what is the point of the European Union?"

And now they want to give carte blanche to American companies, no slouches themselves when it comes to laying waste and avoiding niceties such as corporate rules and regulations.

The whole TTIP concept is yet another illustration of the restricted mindset of EU policymakers.

Their lack of perspective prevents the EU from seeing what an anachronism it truly is – a customs union, a nineteenth century contrivance and accordingly is obsessed with static borders, protective tariffs and the attendant paraphernalia such as mind numbing nomenclatures (i.e. system of names for products that already have names) and oceans of bureaucracy.

Yet both the EU and US seem eager to superimpose this antiquated concept on a world that lives in the twenty first century.

Enter visionaries like Google, Facebook, Oracle, Amazon, SAP etc., who inhabit the future and operate in the clouds from where they can see way past the present. When they encounter meddlesome hindrances from officialdom, they bring to bear their futuristic alchemy which allows them to run rings around the doddering zollverein governments.

Tim Worstall is a Fellow at the Adam Smith Institute, a body which is a leading proponent of Free Trade. In the *Telegraph* (June 2012) under the heading '... *we should declare free trade unilaterally"* he wrote *" the purpose of trade is imports: exports are just the boring stuff we do to be able to afford them ... the only point of trade ... is what we get to enjoy in exchange."*

In other words revert to Laissez Faire, literally "let it be", "allow to do", "don't interfere" – the original definition of Free Trade.

Marquis d'Argenson the French Minister of Foreign Affairs under King Louis XV in 1751 said *"Let it be, that should be the motto of all public powers, as the world is civilised.... That we cannot grow except by lowering our neighbours is a detestable notion! Only malice and malignity of heart is such a principle and our national interest is opposed to it. Let it be, for heaven's sake! Let it be!"*

The EU is incapable of "let it be" not only within its own territory but government ministers, politicians, bureaucrats, church leaders and indeed citizen groups all over Europe take it upon themselves to go way beyond their own borders to vent their righteous indignation and impose their own dubious morality, sanctions and boycotts on whatever countries or individuals they consider not to be living up to their own "exemplary" standards.

Do any of those countries have on their statute books a law of such "malice and malignity of heart" that a subsidised vegetable takes precedence over a human life – or is this just another of the EU's unique achievements?

Before being so quick to judge and criticise others perhaps the sanctimonious Europeans should direct their attention towards the cruel and inhumane laws they export beyond their own jurisdiction but conveniently condone because they profit from them.

These standards led to the tragedy in Lampedusa and many more that didn't get as much publicity. But it is not just refugees who suffer. This ethos is also at the heart of the economic nightmares experienced in every EU country.

Dimitris Christoulas discerned that the devastation of his country stemmed from his government's collaboration with the EU to the detriment the Greek people. With the proposed EU-US Treaty, European leaders now want to impose on their already frazzled citizens yet another outside power which most likely will just increase the torment.

The islanders saw things clearly and shouted "Disgrace", Killers", as well as jeering and booing the President of Europe who was accompanied by the Italian Prime Minister during his inspection of the southern borders of the EU.

"These deaths are on the conscience of Italian and EU politicians" was another Lampedusan cry, pointing to the collusion of the Italian government.

How ironic that only eighteen months earlier Mr. Christoulas, a Greek, should have written *"the Tsolakoglou (collaborationist) government has annihilated all traces of my survival."*

CHAPTER 7

FRANCE + GERMANY = EUROPE
Et les autres? ....De qui parlez-vous?

PART 1: *The French Hustle*

The Great Train Robbery occurred in Britain in 1963. Over GBP £2.6 million was stolen, equivalent to around GBP £46 million in today's value. The incident was dubbed the Crime of the Century but the definition is not strictly true as a much bigger heist took place some thirteen years earlier when France hijacked Europe.

The only similarity is that in both cases the loot has not yet been returned to its original owners.

A gang of fifteen was involved in the Train Robbery but just three French Superheroes pulled off the European caper – The Man With The Plan, The Incredible Scheming Man, and Le Guerrier Formidable.

The Man With The Plan: This was Jean Monnet, a French diplomat and economist who was tasked with getting the post-war European economy going again. In 1943, concerned that European countries were too weak individually to drive pros-perity, he declared that after the war they must form a federa-tion to make themselves into a *"common economic unit."*

In 1950 Jean Monnet and his team conceived the idea of the European Community. He abhorred political conflict and his concepts were designed to be implemented by technocrats (i.e. experts) rather than politicians but it was politicians to whom he had to submit them.

The Incredible Scheming Man: Monnet's Plan when unveiled to the world by Robert Schuman, the French Foreign Minister, somehow had become known as the Schuman Declaration when he announced the inauguration of the European Coal and Steel Community (ECSC).

By now it had become a political instrument specifically geared to strengthening the French economy at Germany's expense and implanting French bureaucracy throughout the Planning Commissariat.

Konrad Adenauer the German Chancellor referred to a letter from Schuman informing him that the main purpose of his proposition was *"eminently political"*

Le Guerrier Formidable: Charles de Gaulle was a prisoner in World War One, having been wounded three times. In between wars he had urged modernisation of the French army which put him at loggerheads with his superiors who had opted for the extravagantly fortified but immovable Maginot Line. In May 1940 when the German attack simply bypassed this static defence, de Gaulle was given command of an armoured division and after initial setbacks he actually managed to breach the German lines but was ordered to withdraw and soon after was appointed undersecretary of war.

With the enemy rolling relentlessly towards Paris and the French leaders in armistice mode, de Gaulle departed France to continue the fight from England.

The pro-Nazi Petain government labelled him a traitor and condemned him to death. De Gaulle's riposte was to brand the Vichy regime as the traitors and he declared himself the only true French government. He tried (unsuccessfully) to involve himself in the liberation of occupied colonial French territories and was manic in his efforts to jockey France into a position of optimum influence after the war at which he was eminently more successful.

Throughout the war he kept demanding equal status from the Allies and his arrogance infuriated the allied leaders both military and civilian. But his single mindedness never wavered.

Winston Churchill wrote *"I resented his arrogant demeanour. Here he was, a refugee from his own country under sentence of death … he had no real foothold anywhere. Never mind: he defied all."* *
*© The Estate of Winston S. Churchill

And so it came to pass that these three Frenchmen were allowed a free hand to redesign Europe. The post-war regulations, patronage and red tape systems which they initiated still govern our lives today.

Jean Monnet had an unparalleled international reputation firstly through working in his family's cognac business then as a diplomat. He became Secretary General of the League of Nations in 1919 but resigned in 1923 to go back into business and finance. In 1934 he helped in the reorganisation of the Chinese railway system.

From 1940 he worked for the British government in the United States procuring war supplies and became an adviser to President Roosevelt. With such a stellar track record there is little doubt that Jean Monnet's proposals would have received a positive reception at the highest level but without Charles de Gaulle the French may not have been allowed to have much influence over their implementation.

At critical junctures both before and during the war France

failed spectacularly to deliver what would be expected of a friend and ally and instead portrayed itself as an enemy.

For example –

Let-down No 1: The Treaty of Versailles was the formal peace settlement at the end of World War One. Britain and USA wanted Germany severely penalised but tempered with leniency in the hope that it would lead to European reconciliation. On the other hand, France wanted Germany permanently weakened and insisted that crippling territorial and financial sanctions be imposed.

The reparations demanded in 1921 amounted to over 132 billion Marks, approximating to GBP £284 billion in 2012 values. John Maynard Keynes and many other prominent economists forcefully expressed the view that this was far too excessive. The American and British leaders concurred and appealed to France to relent.

But the French wouldn't budge. Germany was smothered under such severe conditions which brought together all the necessary ingredients for World War Two.

Let-down No 2: In May 1940 the German army had broken through the French lines and talk of surrender was spreading. With almost 400,000 British soldiers making up the British Expeditionary Force (BEF) and huge amounts of military equipment committed to its defence, Winston Churchill travelled to France to bolster the resolve of the French command but on getting an on- the-spot briefing he was left reeling.

The French army on the front had been destroyed or scattered and when he asked about the strategic reserve he was told there was none. He was *"dumfounded"* – his word. Churchill wrote later that it had never occurred to him that any commanders would have left themselves so vulnerable. He considered the Maginot Line a good basis for defence by using it as *"sally ports for local counterstrokes"* whereas the French regarded it as a gigantic fortress behind which they just had to wait for the enemy to attack.

But the Nazis had invented Blitzkrieg, a new type of warfare which merely circumvented the Maginot Line and left its occupants isolated.

Apart from the defence of France, Britain's overriding objective to have made such a huge commitment of personnel and equipment was to eliminate the possibility of an invasion of the U.K. by defeating the enemy on European soil. The efficacy of the BEF/French military partnership was nullified by the French High Command's refusal to share vital details of its plans and the enemy attack left the French army in tatters.

Churchill was rueful. *"We had a right to know. We ought to have insisted"*

He returned to London on 17th May 1940 in the full realisation that French posturing had placed the BEF in dire peril and Great Britain was left to face the enemy … alone.

Let-down No 3: With the Germans close to Paris and French resolve visibly evaporating, the British prepared a Declaration of Union. This was to give support to Paul Reynaud, the French Prime Minister, who was trying to keep his country in the war despite his cabinet having voted to request armistice terms from the Germans.

The main thrust of the Declaration was that *"France and Great Britain shall no longer be two nations but one Franco-British Union."* Also included was an undertaking that both countries would share responsibility for repairing war devastation on their territory and there would be a single war cabinet during the conflict which will govern *"from wherever best it can."*

This wording was not just reasonable but logical as Churchill had every right to expect that the French leaders would set up government elsewhere and continue the fight. In September 1914, when the Germans had penetrated to within 64 kilometres of Paris, Henri Poincare, the French President moved his government to Bordeaux, nearly 600 kilometres away.

One war and twenty six years later, the British truly believed that both countries would be best served by uniting and merging their interests and Paul Reynaud was indeed encouraged by the proposals. He presented them to his cabinet on 16th June 1940 but the hostile reaction shook him to the core.

The British offer made with sincerity and a good heart was treated with contempt, scorn and sarcasm by many of the French leaders who had now adopted a stance of joining the Nazis rather than fighting them.

Comments in the French cabinet ranged from *"a British ruse to steal its colonies"*, *"being a Nazi province was preferable to becoming a British dominion"*, to the piece de resistance (literal sense only) from Marshal Phillipe Petain, Hero of Verdun, that a union with Britain would be *"fusion to a corpse"*.

Devastated and demoralised by the vehemence of the defeatist faction, Reynaud resigned. The new government immediately asked Germany for armistice terms and six days later, on 22nd June 1940, just forty two days after the initial German attack, France surrendered.

This so-called surrender/armistice was in reality a cosy little arrangement between Hitler and the new French leadership under Marshal Petain. With the promise of relative autonomy, Petain established his collaborationist government in Vichy and wasted no time in trying impress his new Nazi allies.

Let-down No. 4: At the outbreak of World War Two the French Navy ranked number four in the world after US, Britain and Germany. Its efficiency and modernity was due mainly to Admiral Jean-Francois Darlan, the undisputed chief of France's maritime forces.

Long before the situation in France had reached crisis point, Winston Churchill had made a priority to try to persuade Admiral Darlan to commit his fleet to the British cause. Alternatively that the fleet would sail out of French waters to non-combative ports where it would be neutralised.

Should Germany have gained possession of the French ships it would have swung the naval balance of power over-whelmingly against Britain.

The most Churchill could get from his supposed ally was an assurance that they would not fall into German hands.

The day after Reynaud's resignation, Darlan told a senior French commander that he was going to order the ships to British, American or French colonial ports. In the meantime the new Prime Minister, Marshal Petain, had appointed Darlan as Minister of Marine and the following day he announced that he had changed his mind on the grounds that as Minister of Marine he had a different opinion. But he still stood by his assurance that the fleet would not be allowed to fall into German hands.

Winston Churchill was faced with a huge dilemma. Should he trust Darlan to keep his word or was it necessary to remove the threat once and for all? His recent experience with French leaders had not instilled confidence in the trust route so Churchill chose the other option and on 3rd July 1940 the Royal Navy attacked the main body of the French fleet at anchor in Oran (Algiers) and sank a number of warships with the loss of over thirteen hundred French lives.

On 18th June 1940 Churchill announced "… *the Battle of France is over, the Battle of Britain is about to begin."* He was obviously referring to Germany but apart from his unfinished business with Admiral Darlan, it could equally have referred to his own battle with the French leaders.

This battle was of eight weeks duration and in that short time the character traits of the major players were exposed for all to see.

Winston Churchill was scrupulous in submitting his wartime decisions to his war cabinet. Approval was usually unanimous by a cabinet which initially consisted of Churchill himself plus two Conservative and two Labour ministers. Churchill, also made a point of getting out among the British public, especially following an enemy attack, and there was a unity of purpose throughout the nation.

On the other hand, when things got tough, the French leaders changed sides and ran to the enemy. Like the twelfth century Normans who invaded Ireland but became "*more Irish than the Irish themselves"*, the Vichy government was so fervid in implementing German policies of its own accord, it could be said that it was "*more Nazi than the Nazis themselves"* if such a comparative status is possible.

Without being pressed, the Petain government did not delay in setting up anti-Jewish measures, depriving them of citizenship and rights so their property could be easily appropriated. Twenty six concentration camps were established where many died from disease, and starvation. Of a total of 76,000 Jews who were deported from France, only around 2,500 survived.

Pierre Laval, Chief Minister, was responsible for an odious and much hated scheme, sending skilled labourers to Germany in exchange for French prisoners of war in the ratio of three to one. Milice, another of his creations was a police force charged with capturing Jews, Resistance members and left wing activists. Within six months it was over 35,000 strong.

After the liberation of France, judicial judgements on collaborators condemned approximately 120,000 of which 1,500 were death sentences, including Marshal Petain and Pierre Laval. Charles de Gaulle who had become Head of State, commuted Petain's sentence to life in prison but Laval was shot by firing squad in October 1945.

The task of rebuilding post-war Europe fell to the new French leaders, or more accurately they took it upon themselves. They had impressive CVs; Jean Monnet, and Charles de Gaulle had both been involved in the allied war effort and Robert Schumann had been in the French resistance.

But this does not even begin to paint the full picture.

Firstly countless collaborationists, including civil servants, were not even arrested. Of those, many were given amnesty and allowed to hold important positions. Secondly it required a huge bureaucracy for all those war years of stripping Jews of citizenship and re-allocating their possessions, setting up and maintaining concentration camps, planning deportations, providing hundreds of thousands forced labourers, organising political military/police units and the myriad of other essentials needed to run an effective National Socialist state.

In 1997 American academic and historian Robert O. Paxton testifying at the trial of Maurice Papon, a former Vichy official accused of deporting over 1,600 Jews during the war said *"The Nazis needed the French administration....They always complained about the lack of staff."*

While recognising that many individuals had assisted Jews to escape and hide, Mr. Paxton who wrote the seminal "Vichy France: Old Guard and New Order 1940–44" noted that the French state itself had taken part in the policy of their extermination. *"How can one pretend the reverse when such technical and administrative means have been put to this aim?"*

It may have been the leaders who initiated the policies but it needed the armies of "backroom boys" to ensure their enactment. One such backroom boy was a certain Adolf Eichmann whose dossiers were greatly augmented by the sterling work of the French police in voluntarily providing him with extensive files on French and foreign Jews in France and made life much easier for the Gestapo when they went looking for them.

But French officialdom's collaboration with the Nazis went much deeper than administrator level. The vitriolic anti-Semitism, endemic in the French army itself, especially the General Staff (High Command), was exposed to worldwide public scrutiny following the fallout of the notorious Dreyfus Affair in the late 1800's.

The Jewish Captain Alfred Dreyfus was found guilty of spying by means of deliberately fabricated evidence with the full knowledge and participation of his superior officers and certain government ministers. Initially they truly thought they had the right man, but when it became clear that Captain Dreyfus could not have been the culprit, the army took the view that a significant proportion of the French nation would prefer the real traitor to remain at large rather than release the innocent Jew.

In his famous "J'Accuse" open letter to the President of the Republic, (1889) Emil Zola claimed that France was *"sullied by this filth"* and pointed to a certain Lt. Colonel du Paty de Clam as the *"one evil man"* responsible it all.

Over 50 years later, Charles Mercier du Paty de Clam, son of that "evil man" was appointed Head of the Vichy Office of Jewish Affairs whose task was to implement Nazi racial policies. As it transpired, he was not as evil nor as fervently anti-Semitic as his father and showed little enthusiasm for such work, much to the frustration and disappointment of the Nazis. He was the only holder of that position who was not prosecuted in the post-war trials.

De Paty du Clam Junior was a notable exception and in the Rafle duVelodrome d'Hiver, known as the Vel' d'hiv Roundup (Paris) in July 1942 there was no such lack of enthusiasm. French police were joined by officials of SNCF (France's national state-owned railway) when 13,000 Jewish men, women and children were rounded up and put on trains to the death camps. This two day action represented almost one quarter of all French Jews who were murdered in Auschwitz.

Throughout the war, French railway workers and officials found many ways to disrupt and sabotage various train shipments for the Nazis but the Jewish deportations ran like clockwork. By the end of 1944, almost 75,000 Jews had been deported from France.

After the war the technical and administrative means switched focus from shipping people to gas chambers towards planning and inaugurating the European Community.

END of PART ONE

PART 2: ... *and their German Mark*

Nine months after war end, January 1946, Jean Monnet's proposals for the reconstruction of France and Western Europe got under way with the establishment of his Planning Commission which he inundated with French bureaucracy. Vertical committees for Iron and Steel and horizontal committees for labour and problem solving. Devices with fiendish interconnectivity that could not be disassembled without the whole structure crashing.

As if designed to thwart sceptics who may want to introduce reforms in the future which would weaken France's grip on the levers of power. France's masterplan to accelerate its own prosperity was to keep Germany economically weak by taking control of the Saar and Ruhr areas in Germany and appropriating Saar coal to increase their own steel output.

The light at the end of the German tunnel was the promise that the Federal Republic of Germany, created in 1949, would become a sovereign state. For this, the French demanded a limitation on coal and steel production in the Ruhr area which in effect controlled the entire West German economy.

These measures caused anger and dismay among German politicians and Konrad Adenauer was called "Chancellor of the Allies" by the opposition leader but this did not put an end to the demands from Paris. The French did not want an increase in German speakers in the Saar so the Germans were forced to teach French as the first foreign language.

Germany brought an end to its torment in 1951 by agreeing to join the European Coal and Steel Community (ECSC) and in exchange the industrial restrictions were lifted. In 1955 the Federal Republic of Germany (West Germany) became a sovereign state.

This was how the European Union was started and the bullying, totalitarian ethos which was implanted in its system was put to early use. The ECSC was run by an unelected High Authority, which apart from administering the common market, also had the power to shut down coal mines and steel plants by secret decisions made behind closed doors.

The aphorism attributed to Charles de Gaulle that *"Europe is France and Germany: the rest are just the trimmings"* is not fanciful, it is the plain unvarnished truth.

France in the driving seat was able to make the rules to suit its own aspirations. Rule No. 1 was France can suck resources out of Germany to accelerate its own prosperity. It was able to achieve this by convincing the US that such a course was in the interest of military security.

After Germany's unconditional surrender, the Allies ruled, so such decisions were made over its head. In 1949 the first West German government took office headed by a man who was depicted as *"one of the greatest figures of the post-war period."* This description was by Nahum Goldmann in April 1967 following the death of Dr. Konrad Adenauer aged 91. Its significance is that Dr. Goldmann was President of the World Jewish Congress.

Konrad Adenauer opposed the Nazis and was arrested and imprisoned in1934 and again in 1944, this time by the Gestapo, aged 68, accused of involvement in the July Plot to assassinate Hitler.

Obviously incredibly brave and of immensely strong resolve, why, after becoming Chancellor of West Germany, did he allow the French to continue preying on his country? The answer was that he had no choice because the Allies had overall control and the French were very good at whingeing to get their own way.

Nonetheless from 1949, under Dr. Adenauer's leadership, West Germany was able to grow out of its post-war economic and political devastation. He started from scratch on the economy but from minus scratch on the political side. Both Dr. Adenauer's Christian Democratic Union (CDU) and the other political parties were unwilling to alienate the significant percentage of the West German electorate which had once supported the Nazis. There were also powerful lobby groups representing Germans who were expelled or managed to escape from Eastern Europe that the political parties wanted to keep on board.

Therefore, fundamental political decisions had to be tempered with pragmatic gestures to please various segments of the electorate. Just the same as any other long established democracy but Konrad Adenauer managed to achieve this in a few short years.

On the economic front, Dr. Adenauer received a letter from Robert Schuman, the French Foreign Minister, in May 1950, proposing the now famous (or infamous) "High Authority" with supranational powers to control France and West Germany's coal and steel industries. Schuman suggested that this would be the best way to develop their economies and at the same time bring the two countries closer together.

Dr. Adenauer immediately agreed.

In his memoirs, Dr. Adenauer stated that although German, he always felt like a European and had long championed an understanding with France. He further surmised that after 1945, in his view, the comprehensive destruction of Germany's infrastructure effectively removed any threat to France.

He was influenced by a speech that Charles de Gaulle had made in Saarbrucken in August 1945 in which he exhorted the two countries to work together – as Europeans … *"Frenchmen and Germans must let bygones be bygones."* To Dr. Adenauer such sentiments made him feel very positive about Germany's future and his *"hopes for a united Europe."*

Get the picture? These are the building blocks of what is today's EU and right down at foundation level is the unavoidable truth that "Europe is France and Germany: the rest are just the trimmings." And should there be any doubt, the official EU web portal refers to the personalities behind these events as among those who inspired the European Union of today.

To make a United Europe look credible, more than just two countries were needed, so say hello to the first batch of trimmings.

Italy, laid low by the war, couldn't wait to join and the other three were known as Benelux. If New York was so good they named it twice, how does one rate three countries they don't name even once?

Not exactly equivalent status to France and West Germany but trimmings are merely an embellishment and can never have any meaningful input into what the garment they adorn should look like.

Not everyone in the West German government was in agreement with Dr. Adenauer. His Economics Minister, Ludwig Erhard, was unhappy with the terms Dr. Adenauer had agreed for West Germany's membership of the European Economic Union (EEC). An implacable opponent of a planned economy, he protested the very idea of joining a customs union. This put him at odds with Dr. Adenauer who overruled him but still kept him as his Economics Minister – for the full fourteen years of his tenure as West German Chancellor.

And why not? The economic triumph in Germany was Dr. Erhard's handiwork. To those Europeans having to put up with politicians constantly lauding the illusory benefits of the EU, the works of this Ludwig are indeed sweet music.

In 1947 he became economic advisor to General Lucius Clay, military governor of the U.S. zone, and turned conventional economic thinking on its head. In July 1948, on his own initiative, he abolished rationing and put an end to price controls. When a U.S. colonel confronted him for relaxing their rationing system in the middle of a widespread food shortage, Erhard denied relaxing it saying he had *"abolished it!"*

He said that from then on the only rationing ticket would be the deutschmark for which people will work hard to obtain. *"Just wait and see."*

He knew exactly what he was talking about. Without the restrictions of rationing and price control, supply and demand soared and individuals were able to start building their future instead of living from hand to mouth. When he became Dr. Adenauer's Economics Minister, he added tax cuts to his programme of deregulation. The result was the German Economic Miracle.

From the outset, the ECSC needed a hefty bureaucracy, if only to administer and control the Saar and Ruhr areas which was key to France's economic recovery. The ethos of such officialdom and regulation was carried forward in its transition into the EEC and did not fit Dr. Erhard's belief that the economy would not be able to flourish if handicapped by *"seemingly social measures in neighboring fields."*

His attitude was that if the economic policies were successful the need for social policies became less relevant.

He could not stop it coming into existence but he tried to inculcate the European Economic Union with his free market ideas. Politically, General de Gaulle believed in the concept of the nation state and rejected Jean Monnet's ideas on supra-nationalism. So in those days there weren't all those

Euro-busybodies scuttling around creating volumes of meaningless rules to keep themselves in pointless jobs or truckloads of suffocating red tape to hinder enterprise and development.

It was in its early days that EEC activities most closely resembled Free Trade and became a shining example to the world. Other European countries, including Britain, looked on in envy, and clamoured to become members. But they focused only on the de facto situation – on what they saw happening on the ground.

They chose to ignore the de jure, official, main objective which was still at the very heart of the EEC project – creation of a United States of Europe. The protagonists were merely biding their time using the "step by step" approach as recommended by Jean Monnet.

The applicant countries also seemed blind to the sign on the door, which clearly read –

CLUB EUROPE

MAIN ENTRANCE: FRANCE and GERMANY ONLY

TRIMMINGS USE REAR DOOR

In 1960 Britain applied to join and the federalists were all for it. Charles de Gaulle disagreed and barred the Brits from entering. To him, they didn't even rate as trimmings so they couldn't use the rear door either. H. S. Chopra in his book *De Gaulle and European Unity* wrote that his rejection stemmed from the historical and linguistic links Britain had with US and the Commonwealth.

According to Chopra, Monnet wanted Britain as a counterbalance against Germany. De Gaulle did not share Monnet's view that a federal system was the answer. His idea of European Unity was on the pattern of traditional alliances which was more line with Churchill's thinking.

Apparently fear of German domination over Europe was also shared by the Germans themselves.

In an article for the New York Review of Books entitled "The Euro: The Engine That Couldn't", Josef Joffe wrote that Konrad Adenauer, like Willy Brandt and Helmut Kohl, *"knew that Germany was too weak to act alone but too strong for the rest of Europe to leave it alone … When Germany, its power untrammelled, struck out on its own, the result was ever greater disaster."*

This was published December 1997 and sure as eggs is eggs, albeit sixteen years later, (October 2013) the U.S. Report to Congress on International Economic and Exchange Rate Policies claimed that Germany's strong exports were *"destroying the equilibrium of the overall European economy."*

Commentators surmised that the Americans were still smarting from the mobile phone melodrama and when presented with the chance of showing the Germans up, they took it. They obviously didn't stop to consider how it is possible to try to embarrass someone for being successful without actually embarrassing themselves.

Histrionics aside, Germany's sparkling performance had shown the world that at least one country in the Brussels portfolio was not a hopeless dummkopf, so the Eurocrats must have been over the moon.

Wrong!! Germany was guilty of achieving too high a surplus and this type of performance is just not acceptable in the EU so the European Commission also had to warn Germany not to be so successful.

Apparently, "macroeconomic imbalances" arise when a

disorder called "achievement" invades the sickly EU bloodstream and in 2011, guidelines were introduced to counteract this. In simplistic terms, the successful party must not exceed a certain level of surplus unless it makes sacrifices in other parts of its economy to compensate the other Euro deadbeats for being exposed to the trauma of accomplishment.

Having seen how the European experience had made Greece, Ireland, Spain so compliant, one would expect that when ordered by the EU to put a brake on its economic performance, Germany would also fall into line? Wrong again!! Germany not only owns Club Europe but also happens to pay for the other members, so if it decides to ignore the Commission or even make its own rules, who is going to disagree?

When told about an impending warning from Brussels, a German government spokesman said this was unlikely and anyway, surplus was not be the only measure of an economy.

But this kerfuffle was unnecessary because one of the major factors that afforded such export success to Germany was the comparative weakness of the Euro. The same is available to all the other Eurozone countries but despite Germany tying one hand (maybe both?) behind its back in voluntarily handicapping itself by being *"safely locked into European institutions"* (Josef Joffe) it could still outperform all the others put together.

What does that make the rest of the EU? ... a pack of lazy gobshites??

Well, maybe that's a bit harsh.

Still, if Germany is so successful, how come the rest is doing so badly?

As Cassius might have put it – *"The fault dear Brutus, is not in our stars, but in the Euro"*, which makes life much easier for German exporters. Those steely, unyielding, unadulterated components of the pristine Deutschmark were debilitated by being mixed with a hefty dose of former Drachma Greek spendthrifts, a sprinkling of dodgy former Irish Punt bankers, a soupçon of reckless former Spanish Peseta property developers and a pinch of former Italian Lira bunga bunga, thereby weakening the hitherto mighty German currency and the price of its exports.

Unfortunately the blessing for Germany turns out to be a curse to the others because in their case, the reverse applies. Olive oil, agricultural produce, holidays on Greek islands and sunny Mediterranean beaches which used to be so competitive in their old independent currencies, became more expensive when leveraged with German motor cars, high tech engineering, construction products and chemicals.

Charles de Gaulle's dictum, *"the rest are just the trimmings"* was possibly a declaration of bravado on his part, but that doesn't mean it isn't true. It was uttered long before the Euro came into existence and should have been taken as a cautionary warning. Yet the empty-headed politicians tripped over themselves to lock their countries into whatever Germany was signing up for with little more reasoning than "if the Germans think it's good then we must have a piece of it too."

But all substance within EU's orbit is destined to be dragged downwards and a mere twelve months later even the mighty Germany had capitulated to its irresistible gravitational pull. Its powerhouse economic performance had gone into reverse as its manufacturing activity shrank due to deflation and meagre growth in the Eurozone.

The EU, mindful of its duty to appear consistent, duly implemented those policies of rewarding failure and penalising success. A month later in November 2014, because they were doing comparatively better, the British were ordered to pay a surcharge of GBP £1.72 billion so that Germany and

France could get large rebates. And similarly, Italy and The Netherlands were also instructed to pay substantial sums.

Manuel Barroso, President of the European Commission pointed out that these were the rules so no one should be surprised. Rules that ensure that when France and Germany win, they win and even when they lose, they win.*

* This is not the bit Mr. Barroso pointed out. He just mentioned the first bit.

The losers, as always, are ... the trimmings.

On balance, to label the others a pack of lazy gobshites is not really an apt description. A bunch of right eejits seems far more fitting.

END of PART 2

PART 3: *The French Lesson*

Throughout history, France has had an urge to conquer and rule over other countries and used to travel all over the world in pursuit of this goal. Exotic names such as Devil's Island in French Guiana and Dien Bien Phu in Vietnam spring to mind. But it was on their doorstep, in less salubrious Europe, that the last major attempt for French supremacy by military means failed … the details of which Abba so graphically described for posterity.

Even the debacle at Waterloo did not appear to extinguish their craving for domination. Biding their time, over 130 years later, they spotted a post-war opportunity while World War Two was still in progress and wasted no time in plotting and devising their blueprint for French mastery over Europe to be implemented once peace had been delivered.

The victorious Americans and their allies, including Britain, wanted to get back to their own countries as soon as practical, causing them to take France as a partner in the policing and rebuilding of Europe. A big plus may have been the fact that Winston Churchill was a Francophile and made a clear distinction between the ordinary people of France and the perfidious actions of their leaders.

So a wartime ally of the Nazis which had surrendered just six weeks after the first German attack, was invited to sit at the victor's table, was bestowed with the prestige of becoming the fourth occupying power in West Berlin and was handed the continent of Europe on a plate.

"Trente glorieuses" is the term coined by Jean Fourastie, a French demographer, to describe the thirty years of remarkable economic success enjoyed by France from the end of the war until the early nineteen seventies. Then it seemed to run out of steam and while the German half of Europe marched onwards

and upwards, the French half slipped backwards and downwards.

There is nothing unique or remarkable about a country being a roaring success one day and a outright flop the next. Unfortunately for hapless citizens, thanks to their politicians, it happens all the time … all over the world. But only in Europe is the maniacal insistence of leaders to remain joined at the hip to other nations with such proclivity for failure that if one economy goes pop, the rest, in varying degrees of severity, are automatically pulled down too.

After the war, France found itself elevated into the position it had coveted for hundreds of years – master over Europe. The French post-war leaders in the twentieth century, unarmed and without reinforcements, had succeeded where previous rulers, such as Louis XIV in the eighteenth and Napoleon Bonaparte in the nineteenth, both with massive armies and plenty of reinforcements, had failed.

But French propensity for burgeoning government expenditure, continually enlarging an already enormous public sector, flooding enterprise with bureaucracy, red tape and taxes, proved too much a burden for the growth rate to be able to continue indefinitely and it inevitably started to flag.

The sluggishness regrettably turned out to be much longer lasting than the buoyant trend, to the extent that in November 2012 an Economist cover story described France as *"The time bomb at the heart of Europe"*.

France had long forfeited its position to be considered one of the lead countries but in the EU, sycophancy, gullibility and compliance outweigh merit and economic principles. Irrespective of performance, France made sure it would always wield power and influence because at the design stage, it had biased the European infrastructure in favour of French interests.

Alternating the European Parliament between Brussels and

Strasbourg is a prime example. Each month, arrangements have to be made to shift, over seven hundred and fifty MEPs plus assistants, translators etc. from Brussels (Belgium) for a four day plenary session in Strasbourg (France) … and back to Brussels (Belgium) again.

They go by train and more than two thousand storage crates are sent separately by lorry.

The estimated annual cost is around STG £130 million in cash, almost 20,000 tons in carbon dioxide emissions and 317 in empty days of a fully equipped and staffed Parliament building somewhere in France. Add to the pointlessness, the monthly ride on the Euroround about and even the most fanatical EU apostles find it hard not to blush.

"Bonkers" is how Nick Clegg, U.K. Deputy Prime Minister, described it in October 2013 as one of the reforms he would like to see, and who would disagree?

Actually France does. More to the point because it has a veto, even if every other country voted to end it, the Strasbourg carousel will always remain at France's pleasure. When the issue was raised during the presidency of Nicolas Sarkosy he stated it was "non-negotiable."

End of story … next reform please?

Who wouldn't want to see the end of the diabolical Common Agricultural Policy (CAP) of which France was one of the founder members. In 2011 CAP paid out an astronomical fifty eight billion euros to individual farmers within the EU but details of the recipients and amounts is not available.

A ruling of the Court of Justice of the European Union stated that in the case of CAP, the usual rules on transparency were invalid. This opened the door for states in receipt of CAP payments (i.e. taxpayers' money) to hide details of how much they got.

Some governments took this as an opportunity not to publish

any figures at all, and others, including France, formatted the information in such a manner that it would need a financial Enigma machine to decipher. As for the U.K., it simply eradicated the names of some of the larger beneficiaries.

Who wouldn't want to run a million miles to escape this contemptible setup led by people with such a despicable outlook on right and wrong, but according to the Deputy Prime Minister in May 2014, anyone who proposed that the U.K. should quit the EU was *"deeply unpatriotic."*

A patriot is one who expresses national loyalty so his accusation brings to mind three things –

1. The aim of the EU is to eliminate the nation state, so the contrary is true.
2. As one who advocates and condones his country being ruled by foreigners from a foreign land, was it not the Deputy Prime Minister and his cohorts who were being "deeply unpatriotic."
3. Dimitris Christoulas referred to his EU-chummy government as *"traitors of this country."*

With Germany shooting up into the stratosphere and France falling in the opposite direction, the joint facade has been torn asunder and the twenty six other nations, the trimmings, lie scattered and in disarray all over Europe. Could have been easily avoided – they just had to quit the EU, or not join at all like Iceland, but the pitiful European leaders are incapable of running their own countries without instructions from Brussels.

Although Charles de Gaulle resigned as President of France almost fifty years ago, his description of the lackey nations of the EU is as pertinent today as it ever was.

Trimmings indeed …

FIN

CHAPTER 8

Revolution is inevitable in a state which is devoid of decency

During the Battle of Britain, in 1940, Winston Churchill made a point of visiting places that had been bombed and interacting with those who were affected. One of these visits took him to Ramsgate, a seaside town, thirty three miles north of Dover in the county of Kent.

He writes in his memoirs *"A small hotel had been hit. Nobody had been hurt, but the place had been reduced to a litter of crockery, utensils and splintered furniture. The proprietor, his wife and the cooks and waitresses were in tears. Where was their home? Where was their livelihood?"*

What he did next is quite breathtaking.

On his way back to London, he wrote to the Chancellor of the Exchequer instructing *"... that all damage from the fire of the enemy must be a charge upon the State and compensation to be paid in full and at once."*

The principle being *"... that the burden would not fall alone on those whose homes or business premises were hit, but would be borne evenly on the shoulders of the nation."*

There was consternation. The Treasury was worried about the *"indefinite character of this obligation ... .but I pressed hard and an insurance scheme was devised in a fortnight ..."*

From May 1941, with no air raids for three years, the Treasury made money. But the rocket and "doodle bug" phase towards the end of the war, reversed this, resulting in eight

hundred and ninety million pounds being paid out. Winston Churchill's comment? *"I am very glad this was so."* *
*© The Estate of Winston S. Churchill

Churchill, highly knowledgeable in the ways of war, was aware of two crucial factors on which the survival of Britain depended. Firstly, he knew that without air superiority, Germany could not launch a successful invasion by sea. Consequently the German objective in the Battle of Britain was primarily about the destruction of the Royal Air Force (RAF), in order to give them that edge.

Until the Luftwaffe was finally overcome, he constantly fretted about the outcome of the war and at the time of his visit to Ramsgate this was by no means clear. He could have shrugged off the bombed out hotel along the lines *"what a shame but these things happen in war"* and who would have thought any less of him?

But high on Winston Churchill's priorities was to maintain decency in the face of the enemy's depravity. Decency ... respect for human dignity ... accepting responsibility.

After the war (fifty nine years after, to be exact) this was enshrined in "A Constitution for Europe – the founding principles of the Union." Number one in the Values of the Union category is *"respect for human dignity"* and *"sustainable development"*, *"aiming at full employment"* and to promote the *"well-being of its people"* are among the Objectives of the Union.

A further five years later, in 2009, the Euro crisis started hitting home, and austerity measures caused "respect for human dignity" to be dumped, along with sustainable development, full employment and even well-being of the people, as millions of European citizens were economically wiped out

not from "fire of the enemy", but that of their own governments, typifying the character of the European Union – big on
promising, small on keeping them.

In November 2014, Pope Francis spoke to the European
Parliament (the one in Strasbourg) and described the EU as
being "downright harmful" to its own people. He was critical of a political system that oppressed migrants, abandoned
the young and elderly and ... wait for it ... "betrayed human
dignity."

The whole idea, point, purpose, aim, justification, reason,
excuse for the EU is to bring peace and prosperity to the
citizens of Europe. Instead it has delivered hardship, poverty,
deprivation and widespread dissension.

Pope Francis made it crystal clear just how far off target
they were. And how did the MEPs react to the Pope's stinging
denunciation?

They kept applauding his remarks!

Surreal or what?

Shades of Homer Simpson? Dohhhhhhh ...

Despite all the criticisms, protests and demonstrations the
EU leaders stuck to their guns and sure enough, one by one,
the stricken countries started showing signs of recovery. In
July 2014 it was joyously announced that Italy was gaining
on Ireland and Spain which were then among Eurozone's top
performers.

On the way to becoming a star EU achiever, Ireland also
picked up the accolade of topping the European league of
household unemployment. In 2010, there was an unemployed
adult in one in five households. This was more than double the
Eurozone average.

Although Spain and Greece had higher overall unemployment rates, their household unemployment of 10% and 7.5%

respectively was outstripped by Ireland's resounding 20%.

This inert statistic was given a kiss of life by Irish Independent journalist Carol Hunt in an article (June 2014) entitled *"A tale of two Irelands, but one of them is pure fiction."* The Ireland of the Taoiseach (Irish Prime Minister), Enda Kenny, is "The Lovely Ireland" where jobs were secure, mortgages low and everything is *"coming up roses ..."*

But in her Ireland, she finds it hard to sleep, worrying about surviving after paying the monthly bills and pondering how those in the households of that 20% sector (her figure is 22%) in the majority of which there are children, can get by.

Debt as a cause of suicide is still "a huge issue" and an estimated 10,000 are in imminent danger of losing their homes to the banks but the Taoiseach keeps referring to safe jobs, growth, exceeding targets, and Carol Hunt wonders if anybody told him about the other Ireland that she has to live in.

The founder of one of many Irish organisations trying to support and guide those in economic despair, told Ms. Hunt that he had been trying for two and a half years to get a meeting with the Taoiseach to tell him the facts.

Such depressing and negative underlying circumstances makes one wonder what exactly is the criteria for a "top performer" in EU terms?

In April 2012, the Spanish Prime Minister said there was no money to pay for public services because *"we have spent so much ..."* In November 2012 the European Commission gave Spain access to forty billion euros to help out its banks, yet, the following year, suicides were reported from many parts of Spain for reasons ranging from not being able to get enough to eat to having homes repossessed as a result of losing jobs.

Then in July 2014, the year it became a Eurozone "top performer", it was reported that "tens of thousands" of

Spaniards were emigrating to Britain following the more than eight thousand who had moved there the previous year. Other notable points from Spain's CV were tens of thousands losing their homes, 25% overall unemployment and fifty per cent of Spaniards between the ages of eighteen and twenty four out of work.

Despite this carnage, in early 2015 following improved economic figures Spain was dubbed "The Poster Boy for Recovery in Europe." A few months later Spain could have become EU Poster Boy for Vacant Houses if such an accolade had existed.

In June 2015 it was reported that a third of all the empty homes in Europe were to be found in Spain. This was due to a 'blitz" of evictions which is the real story behind the EU spin.

The other EU pin-up didn't seem to fare much better when in June 2014 Mr. Jans Weidmann, Head of the Bundesbank cast doubt on Italy's commitment to Eurozone recovery. He was reacting to the Italian Prime Minister's reference to the EU as an *"old boring aunt"*.

Despite this unflattering description that same month Italy was said to be hot on the heels of EU "top performers" Spain and Ireland. Yet in 2013, Italy experienced a forty percent increase in suicides, over 100,000 companies were involved in insolvency talks, and in 2014 Italy's Youth Unemployment rate was over 40%.

Although not on the "top performer" list, January 2014 saw Greek ministers *"in a bullish mood"* but not so bullish was the stark overall Greek unemployment rate of over 27% (April 2014) and 56% for those up to the age of 24 who did not have a job. Suicide was still a feature with an estimate that half was due to the austerity measures. A World Health Organisation review in 2013 reported that some Greeks were deliberately injecting themselves with HIV to avail of government benefits for those affected.

In a Sunday Times feature (Sept. 2013) entitled *"It's Almost Impossible to Pay the Bills",* Constantina Grammenou, unemployed, 39 years old and living in Athens, wrote that school for her thirteen year old son started in October last year, instead of September, because of lack of teachers. *"This year it could be worse."* She reckons that Greece is now experiencing poverty on the scale of the post-war years and looks to the god of ancient Greek tragedy whose role was to offer solutions. *"He is my only hope."*

In each case, the so-called "economic success" appears to be built on ignoring and trying to conceal the fall-out from the failure of the previous so-called "economic success." Despite the EU claim to have prevented war, these casualties are innocent victims of an operation gone horribly wrong … collateral damage, plain and simple, … of gargantuan proportions.

When calamity befell that small family-run hotel in Ramsgate, Winston Churchill's instinct was to offer support to those stricken citizens. Despite the odds, "respect for human dignity" was still a high priority.

By contrast, the EU barons wrote a constitution, gave it a hifalutin title and set out a series of high minded values and objectives. Then they patted themselves on the back for being such paragons of virtue and as soon as these values were most needed they turned their backs on them.

Their instinct was to save themselves and their fellow leaders, at any cost, in the hope that they could muddle through until the "Big Idea" finally prevailed and then all those Utopian concepts would just fall into place.

But this still looks as unlikely as ever.

How on earth can ordinary citizens break away from these

despots that so blight their lives?

Thomas Paine, an Englishman, put forward the notion that revolution is an allowable option if a government fails to protect the rights and interests of its people. He stated that the aim of revolutions is for *"a change in the moral condition of governments."*

He proposed this in his book "Rights of Man", written in 1791, in support of the French Revolution (1787 to 1789). He had corresponded with Thomas Jefferson and William Franklin following the American Revolution (1765 to1783) regarding the U.S. Constitution and George Washington said that Americans owed their liberty to Thomas Paine more than to any other man.

What occurred in America and France over two hundred years ago determined how citizens in those countries still live today and showed that a revolution which succeeds in merely sweeping away the status quo is not a satisfactory result. It must also establish a durable and long-lasting new order in its place.

A more recent revolution in Egypt which managed the first but not the second-stage, occurred during the so-called Arab Spring.

All these revolutions were brought about by the citizens of different continents, each with a differing culture and language, yet in each case the motive was exactly the same, namely to kick out those who misused the power they exercised over them.

Was this sheer co-incidence or is there a thread common to all human beings all over the world?

The American economist and diplomat, J.K. Galbraith, in his book *American Capitalism*, first published in 1952, invented the term "countervailing power", referring to restraint of private power in the market. Hitherto, economists had attributed this to competition such as a manufacturer competing against other manufacturers who were on the same side of the market.

J.K. Galbraith put forward that restraint on a manufacturer's power did not arise from competitors but rather from customers or suppliers who were on the opposite side of the market.

Although he applied his proposition to economics and commerce, one of his working examples does have a similarity to politics. He observed that generally where there are powerful corporations one finds the strongest trade unions thus providing the workers with the protection of countervailing power.

Conversely as farmers did not have much power over their workers there were not unions of comparable power in American agriculture.

In a similar vein, an electorate does not feel threatened under a benign government so it tends to be sheep-like, even apathetic. But when a regime exploits its citizens, this causes them to want to protect themselves … it's only natural.

Hence the seeds of countervailing power are planted which will ultimately result in either a curb on the government's power or its ultimate downfall.

The political opposition parties cannot fill the role because they are the same side of the "market" as the ruling party. The opposite side is the ordinary citizens and when the limit of their tolerance is breached, their anger is directed to the source of their problems.

The French had a monarchy for over 1300 years before the revolution removed it. Britain was over 200 years in India and around 180 in America before the Indians and Americans managed to get them to leave. The Mubarak government that preceded Mohammed Morsi had lasted 29 years but it took only one year for a revolution to remove Mr. Morsi.

Timespans varying from just twelve months to more than a millennium which shows that there is no fixed timeframe but ultimately all were very angry events. Generally, it depends on how long an aggressive and intrusive regime is able to keep forcing its people to live under conditions which are manifestly in contradiction to man's natural inclinations.

Nowhere is this more evident than in Europe itself. Each EU country, at some-time in its history, has experienced revolution of some sort, although in many cases the government managed to stay in place. To those who may have wondered where the term "Arab Spring" originated, the Revolutions of 1848 involving more than fifty European countries, was also known as the "Spring of Nations."

As has been shown repeatedly, even the greatest empires are ultimately brought down by the citizens' innate desire for self-determination. They don't want interfering busybodies telling them how to run their lives ... but then, who does?

Despots have always ignored history and today's tyrants are no different. Despite the human misery caused by the countless economic disasters of their making, the European leaders are so disconnected from the effects of their bungling that they truly believe they are doing a great job and revolution is the last thing on their minds.

Unfortunately there is one problem with this ... well ... make that millions of problems. In 2012, according to the EU itself there were over twenty five million people out of work of which around five million were aged between 18 and 25. Brussels talked of an economic and social disaster caused by "a lost generation."

This would have come as no surprise to Thomas Paine. He had written over 200 years previously, *"the uncivilised state of the European governments is injurious to commerce."* Pity no one heeded him because despite splurging billions of euros and promising measure after measure to try to rectify the situation, in 2014, two years later, Eurostat estimated there were still around twenty five million unemployed. Such is progress in the EU.

These millions are living with little hope of a future for themselves or their children, while the very people who caused their predicament are living in the lap of luxury. What is a citizen supposed to do?

Scenes of citizens in European cities, angered by the terms of some financial rescue package, trying to storm their Parliaments are now fairly commonplace. Did they have a plan to overthrow the government or would they have just smashed up the Parliament building had they managed to break through? One way or another, such demonstrations are hardly a revolution.

Yet the circumstances surrounding the riots are highly significant because without the bailout the country would have run out of money. If the various governments had failed to pass the austerity legislation through their parliament one can only speculate the full extent of what might have unfolded.

Although not an exact comparison, there is a working example from an experience in America.

The deadline for the United States Congress to increase its debt ceiling was 30th September 2013 in order for the US government to continue raising money to run the country. There was no agreement, and on 1st October 2013 extreme action was taken in order to conserve what funds remained.

The measures entailed shutting down government offices, 700,000 workers, one third of the federal workforce, were instructed to stay at home (without pay), most national parks, museums, federal buildings and services closed, pensions and other benefit payments delayed.

Those who had to keep working included military personnel and border security guards. The shutdown lasted just over two weeks during which the country remained relatively calm. Obviously the citizens were not overly incensed with the closure of museums and parks, so the Americans emerged unscathed (apart from an even higher debt) from a crisis which they both created and resolved all by themselves.

Not so the Europeans.

Unlike America, those EU states that get into financial difficulties have to prostrate themselves (the diplomatic term is negotiate), before the fearsome sounding Troika*. True to its fearsomeness, the Troika then subjects the hapless citizens of that country to excruciating conditions in order for the wretched politicians who caused the problems in the first place, to obtain the wherewithal to keep their countries running.

*** Troika = EU + European Central Bank + International Monetary Fund**

With tempers running high all around Europe, should a bailout fail, a government incapable of paying, among others, its security forces, may present too tempting an opportunity for disgruntled citizens to let pass.

Public unrest can occur for the most obscure reasons or even for no good reason at all, as the U.K. found out to its discomfiture in August 2011. Disturbances occurred in Tottenham, North London following the death of a local who was shot dead by police. This escalated to widespread riots in over a dozen other London boroughs and cities such as Birmingham, Bristol and Manchester and several smaller towns.

Pretty soon it had just become a pretext for looting, wanton destruction of property and businesses, the momentum being maintained by "copycat violence." Disturbances in so many areas of London resulted in the Metropolitan Police running out of trained riot police. Reinforcements were bussed in from other parts of the U.K. and after almost a week of chaos, officialdom had once again managed to regain control.

In May 2013, Jacques Attali a senior French Socialist, warned that if President Hollande failed to introduce reforms to reverse the country's decline, France would be doomed to *"turmoil and revolution."*

Turmoil probably, but revolution how? France is renowned for managing civil disturbances. In other EU countries where serious rioting occurred, as with the U.K., their systems coped, so street violence as a means to anything is proving rather futile throughout Europe.

A revolution does not have to be a Bastille style storming of public buildings. "A complete change" also fits the definition which in political terms could be the sweeping away of the established order making way for radical new policies. So Mr. Attali's words may yet prove prophetic.

Aggrieved citizens by merely exercising their right to vote have already started the momentum which could break the EU stranglehold over its member states and the turbulence is likely to spread well beyond the borders of France. The difference this time was that their votes went to parties that were as angry as they were about the way the EU affected their lives.

The European Parliament election in May 2014 saw almost a third of the seats falling to a mixture of far right, hard left, nationalist, anti-immigration and simply anti-EU parties. The two main winners were France's National Front and Britain's UKIP with twenty four MEPs each, an increase of 700%and 85% respectively.

Before the elections, the EU leaders were well aware of

an impending backlash and although hoping that it would not materialise, they were not particularly concerned. Under the headline, *"Voting will not change Europe's power balance"*, Wolfgang Munchau wrote in the Financial Times (5/5/14) that despite the powers of the parliament increasing with each treaty, due to the dynamics in the EU, *"the council is becoming ever stronger."*

What say the voters? Who cares – Brussels rules O.K.?

If it actually transpires that the new MEPs have little or no impact it doesn't really matter because a solution will never be found through the European Parliament. The real significance of the elections is the upheaval to voting patterns all around Europe.

Despite the politicians trying to convince otherwise, Europe's existence does not depend on the EU. On the contrary, it is the EU that endures at Europe's pleasure. The European elections of 2014 showed that very large numbers of people in the member countries were finding that association anything but pleasurable.

In France, U.K. and Denmark around 25% of the votes went to anti-EU parties. In Italy, Austria, Netherlands, Sweden, Hungary and Greece it varied from 10% to around 20%. Should these figures be reflected in the national elections of member states, the Brussels elite would not be feeling so smug and complacent.

In a number of countries the extremists have gained enough traction to be an integral part of the political scenery and in France, National Front is one such party. On the fringes for many years, its new leader, Marine Le Pen, toned down some of its more extreme policies but by remaining relentless against the EU, Euro and immigration, was able to bring it mainstream.

In 2013 she said that if she became president she would

pull France out of the Euro. In 2014 surveys showed that Marine Le Pen would beat President Hollande if a presidential election were held at that time. Should her upward progress continue until 2017, when the actual elections are scheduled, the Euro, along with all the other EU appurtenances, would be on decidedly wobbly ground … certainly much wobblier than at present.

Those anti EU parties which adhered to their full blown xenophobic and racist policies did not make as much advancement but nonetheless managed to establish a beachhead. Their number of seats is small and by no means secure so should the major parties heed the voters and amend their policies accordingly they could conceivably push them back into the sea.

The rise of the extremist parties is fuelled mainly by two facets – the EU being over intrusive in national government and its policy of uncontrolled immigration. Soft pedalling on these issues would probably forestall the opposition's rampant progress but being sensible is not compatible with the EU's imperious ethos.

Europhiles have a simple, straightforward philosophy. "We are never wrong. Just get out of our way." Even after the bashing he got in his own country, Manuel Valls, the French Prime Minister, with jaw dropping head in the sand perspective said *"Europe remains a magnificent project."*

Oy!! You're not listening!! The punters don't agree – they think it's a rubbish project.

The politicians were just as ostrich-like on immigration. Citizens probably just want to see the numbers regulated in accordance with their country's capacity to absorb and accommodate the influx. Seems reasonable.

In November 2014 "a close ally" of Mrs. Merkel, decreed that the principle of free movement of persons was not negotiable.

To avoid any possible misunderstanding, he followed up by adding *"this is a clear message."* Definitely unreasonable.

To the general public the message that clearly came across was that the European legislators had lost the run of themselves and the only protection on offer was from the extremists. Although the EU leaders are dismissive of them being able to exert much influence in the European Parliament they could become quite an irritant should they manage halfway decent results at their national elections.

Almost all EU countries use Proportional Representation for their elections and although the system may broaden the representative nature of a parliament, it also means that one party is unlikely to get an overall majority. This opens opportunities for fringe parties with very small voting bases to horse-trade themselves to seats in government.

During the Weimar Republic (Germany 1919 to 1933) the Nazis used PR to great effect and built their voting share from 2.6% to 37% in less than ten years, after which they had manoeuvred themselves into a position where they were able to abolish elections. Adolph Hitler garnered support from across a broad range of the population by capitalising on their fears and desires arising from Germany's circumstances.

Is it reasonable to equate today's situation to what happened in Germany over eighty years ago?

Compare then and now –

WEIMAR REPUBLIC	**EUROPEAN UNION**
Conditions leading up to Third Reich	**Conditions in many EU countries at time of European Elections 2014**
Foreign governments control over crucial national decisions	*Foreign governments control over crucial national decisions*
Demands of the Allies stripping national pride	*Demands of the EU stripping national pride*
Weak, ineffective political leaders	*Weak, ineffective political leaders*
Basic living costs unafford-able for growing numbers	*Basic living costs unafford-able for growing numbers*
Mass unemployment	*Mass unemployment*
Rampant antisemitism	*Rampant antisemitism*

Notice any similarities?

In a further parallel with the Weimar Republic, millions around Europe have today turned to political parties which, like the Nazis, offer extreme solutions to their problems. In their desperation, citizens have set aside reservations about the less tasteful policies and the result is the huge increase in the Nasti Parties around Europe.

More attention should have been paid to what Dimitris Christoulas had written a good two years earlier *"since my advanced age does not allow me a way of dynamically reacting … I see no other solution than this dignified end to my life."*

Such harrowing words scream out that things are grievously wrong.

CHAPTER 9

Taxation is the fuel of politicians. Without it they can go nowhere

In December 2000 Pierre Fortin, Professor of Economics at the University of Quebec, Montreal published a study entitled "The Irish Economic Boom: Facts, Causes and Lessons." The title page further states "This paper has been prepared for Industry Canada."

Industry Canada is the centre of microeconomic policy expertise of the Canadian Government. Why on earth would it commission a study on an island country one hundred and forty times smaller and with a population about one tenth of that of Canada?

Because *"the astounding Irish employment boom has had no parallel in post-war Europe"* as Professor Fortin observed in his report. There was an underlying concern about the economic gap between Canada and the USA and presumably he was trying to ascertain if there were any lessons to be learned from the Irish experience.

Professor Fortin identifies four main components to the Irish strategy. The first three were commercial, industrial and tax policy. The fourth, education was always deeply embedded in the Irish psyche so it can hardly be called part of a strategy.

Covering commercial and industrial policy he gives a number of fairly scholarly reasons for Ireland's twenty four year-long productivity boom but strip away the infrastructure details and it really boils down to workers being equipped with the latest technology.

Which leaves the question "how do we get the latest technology to come to our country?" so the last policy, tax is not just important but crucial.

Professor Fortin notes that Irish tax policy was well up for it having been *"strongly supportive of business investment for several decades."* This is true but it doesn't convey the full extent of the commitment to business friendly taxes by the Irish politicians of that era.

While other countries were working according to traditional tax strategies Ireland was mulling over the issue of EPTR – Export Profits Tax Relief which according to Frank Barry of Trinity College Dublin first saw the light of day as early as 1945! In his paper "Foreign Investment and the Politics of Export Profits Tax Relief 1956" published in 2011, he traces the evolution of partial and conditional tax relief in 1956 to 100% tax exemption in 1971.

The remarkable feature is that the initial bill for tax relief on "export expansion" in 1956 was introduced by the Taoiseach (Prime Minister) John A. Costello of the Fine Gael party. The full tax remission on exports was passed by the government under the leadership of Sean Lemass of Fianna Fail – two opposing political parties but both at one on the issue of low taxes even to level of zero in order to attract industry to their country.

Conditions in the Ireland of those days were graphically described by Frank McCourt in his book *Angela's Ashes* about his upbringing in the slums of pre-war Limerick and were still fairly prevalent in the 1950's. There were tenements spread around Dublin. These were large decaying old buildings over-populated with large families described in a TV documentary as living in squalor, poverty, malnutrition, rampant disease and a higher infant mortality rate than London.

When Sean Lemass succeeded Eamonn de Valera as Prime Minister of the Republic of Ireland in 1959 the economy was in deep crisis and around thirty thousand Irish citizens were emigrating each year. This represented about one per cent of the population so as well as having to tackle the appalling social conditions he needed to come up with something dramatic to be able to stem such a haemorrhaging of his people.

This was austerity with a vengeance but as events showed, he was well up to the challenge. Building on the work of the previous administration he put together teams of academics, business people and administrators of the type who could think outside the box. The measures that were introduced electrified not only those at home, but also induced large and small corporations from around the world to set up operations in Ireland.

The incentives included generous set up grants, assistance with marketing and research and many other fringe benefits but the feature which stood head and shoulders above all the others was the EPTR.

This attracted overseas companies as diverse as a German manufacturer of giant cranes which set up in 1958 in Killarney to a manufacturer from Chicago who went to Sligo in 1962 to make weighing scales. It should be emphasised that to avail of the low tax regime such factories were committed to exporting their total production and despite the fact that Ireland was not in the Common Market until 1973 most of them thrived which may lead one to surmise that not only politicians but also industrialists were made of much sterner stuff in those days.

Such a high degree of emigration caused significant population shifts with mainly young people moving away from their villages to look for work in larger towns or cities. But the government incentives applied equally to home industry so entrepreneurs started setting up industries in their own locale and in 1971 when zero tax on profits from exports came into force an extra impetus was given to the industrial development of Ireland.

Today's politicians speak about taxation as if it was some miraculous gift to humanity. Countless books have been written about taxation, many incomprehensible even to tax experts let alone the ordinary taxpayer but Sean Lemass's team focused on two big questions, how do you get foreign wealth creators to invest in Ireland and how do you get Irish wealth creators to invest in their own country?

The answer was blindingly simple – promise not to take away their wealth.

Murray N. Rothbard the American historian (1926–1995) said *"Taxation is theft ..."* He depicts it as a mandatory expropriation of citizens' property.

So tax is quite easy to explain.

ALL YOU NEED TO KNOW ABOUT TAX IN LESS THAN 100 WORDS

Dick Turpin, the English highwayman, stopped coaches on the open road and told travellers he was going to take their money.

Jesse James, the American outlaw, boarded trains and told passengers he was going to take their money.

Politicians all over the world stand up in Parliament and tell citizens they are going to take their money.

Dick Turpin and Jesse James carried out their threat immediately so it was robbery and against the law.

Politicians pass legislation beforehand then they take their money. This makes it legalised robbery and not against the law.

Boiling it down, tax can be defined as – OTHER PEOPLES' MONEY (OPM)

Some might say, 'Big deal, our money, other peoples' money. What's the difference?'

There is a world of difference.

In December 2014 Denmark's Margrethe Vestager, EU Competition Commissioner investigating tax deals between certain member states and various international corporations is reported to have said that she would like taxation to be fair.

Wouldn't we all, but one cannot be fair or unfair with oneself so it pre-supposes a two way deal.

On the taxpayers' side all citizens and companies have to account for their income and all expenditure must be verified. This is money you have earned, and every penny must to be detailed to allow the taxman to calculate how much he can take from you to put in the OPM fund.

In return the EU showed that it was not at all interested in fairness when in May 2015 MEPs voted by a margin of ten to one to keep their allowances secret, in effect absolving themselves from any accountability. A more outright circumstance of unfair would be hard to find. How about Ms. Vestager extending her "fair" tax investigation to MEPs?

"Oh look, is that a pig I see flying over the European Parliament?"

Despite not playing fair themselves politicians seem to

have no qualms in exhorting everyone else, especially multi-nationals to pay their *"fair share of taxes"* but there is no such thing. You don't go into a shop to buy a book and see on the label £5.00 plus "fair share" of VAT or Sales Tax. There are only taxes that are legally due, end of story. So why are the politicians making such a fuss?

Their problem is that Brussels' continued existence depends on OPM and with little economic growth and result-ant difficulties they have to keep finding new targets so in August 2013 the uncovering of an abundant source of hitherto untapped riches must have seemed like manna from heaven – but only to the French. It was not until May 2014 that the English speaking world was able to share the thoughts and calculations of Thomas Piketty from his book *Capital in the Twenty First Century*.

Although around 700 pages, the nub is that the wealthy are getting wealthier and to narrow the inequality gap the wealthy should have their wealth taxed significantly.

Politicians with socialist leanings all over the world could hardly contain their excitement. Not only had it been shown that capitalism is a bad thing but they also got a fix on a whole new treasure trove of taxes.

No one was asking what had happened to the countless billions that had already been transferred from individuals and companies into the EU coffers over many decades and yet Europe continues to be mired in deep economic and social difficulties. With such spectacular failure why should the next countless billions be any better?

The very fact that today's society is in such a state as to become the subject matter of such a book is a self-evident truth that this approach does not work.

Taking money from the wealthy and giving it to those

less well-off is not a solution but an extension of the problem because old wealth is only being recycled and the money that is poured over the problem is merely a static ingredient. The participation of an entrepreneur is needed to activate it in order to create new wealth.

Hence the alternative to socialism is individualism. Land, Labour and Capital are the elements of Capitalism and the entrepreneur is the individual who brings the whole process to life. Socialism is a man-made doctrine whereas capitalism is just a depiction of how man made things.

Unlike socialism, capitalism is not a movement and if an entrepreneur messes up it is because he has mismanaged some of its elements. To say *"capitalism has failed"* is as ridiculous as getting a bad meal in a restaurant and claiming *"cookery has failed."* In both cases it is merely that the practitioner was not very good at his trade or maybe just had an off day.

Bearing in mind their own track record, socialists are in no position to condemn such people for having a go. For a master-class in posturing one should take a look at France, especially the curious incident of Pacte de Responsabilite (Responsibility Pact).

In March 2014 French trade unionists and employers' organisations signed a pact under which employers would create more jobs and in return the government would cut business tax. It was initiated by French President Francois Hollande and had been described as the largest social compromise to the country for decades. This is seriously encouraging and although it doesn't go far enough it at least addresses both sides of the problem.

Prime Minister Manuel Valls proclaimed *"j'aime l'enterprise"* and Economy Minister Emmanuel Macron suggested that France might scrap the legal requirement for a

35 hour working week which apparently is not sufficient for workers to cover the costs of their old age.

Another huge impediment is the Code de Travail, the compendium of French employment rules, which contains 3,600 pages of rules. It weighs two kilos (only 500 gms in 1990) and a large number of inspectors are employed to ensure that the rules are enforced

These are the factors most responsible for employer reluctance to give employment and any reforms can only improve things so what happened?

The suggested exemptions to the 35-hour week were greeted with a furious outcry from "dissenting socialists". The office of the "enterprise loving" Mr. Valls came out immediately with a statement that the government had no intention of going back on the legal length of the working week. For good measure a trade union leader said that the government had made a mistake and the subject was closed … and that was from a moderate union.

Nearly three weeks later in September 2014 Mr. Valls warned his Socialist Party that they had six months to save the economy but did not mention the urgency to install a viable working week. How could he? Hadn't he been told by a union leader that the matter was closed? The crushing book of rules wasn't even on the radar.

A month later more uproar when the French were told they will have to cut holidays, so that's not on either. In October 2014 Mr. Valls told his party that they had made a strategic error by not telling the French people the true condition of the country. It seems as if he was unwilling to annoy fellow socialists so he stayed well away from the problems and in that context his speech seemed to have been a great success as there were no reports of uproar or fury – but the problems still remained unaddressed.

Someone who was not impressed with these shenanigans was Maurice Taylor boss of an American tyre factory who had been in negotiations to purchase a "doomed" French tyre factory in Amiens which employed over one thousand people. He walked away from rescuing the factory in November 2014 ridiculed French laws and the demands of trade unions saying that France should become communist. He further suggested that if the unions think they are so smart then why don't they buy the factory themselves?

Is it any wonder that the growth rate of capital exceeds that of the economy and the wealthy are getting wealthier? In this the land of Piketty, who cares if another factory closes when we can always tax the wealthy to make up for it? That is, if they stick around long enough.

If you want to develop your economy you don't alienate people like Maurice Taylor. On the contrary, you make it as investor friendly as possible and low taxes are imperative. The studies on Ireland's early economic development show that it got so much right so why did it all go so badly wrong?

Up to 1973 when Ireland joined the European Economic Community it had to use its own money plus that which it could attract by its own affordable incentives. The growth in the Irish economy up to that time was organic, that is, what it was able to achieve from its own existing efforts and resources.

Following EEC membership, Ireland received 44 billion euros from the Common Agricultural Policy and 17 billion in Structural Funds between 1973 and 2008. Growth rocketed but the rapid infusions of such colossal amounts of money into its system seem to have had a genetically modifying side effect and in 1997 Ireland found itself transformed into a Celtic Tiger. Hitherto tigers had been indigenous to Asia.

Notwithstanding, the government encouraged even greater sums of money to be pumped into the economy and bank lending rose from 5.5 billion euros in 1999 to over 96 billion euros in 2007 and a year later the Celtic Tiger transmuted into a PIIG.*

*PIIGS – acronym for Portugal, Ireland, Italy, Greece and Spain all allowed their country's debts to get out of control.

From muck to muck in three generations is a pithy way of describing the failure of successors to maintain the accomplishments of the trailblazing first generation. In 2013 over 35,000 Irish nationals emigrated so despite splurging almost 160 billion euros of Other Peoples' Money, Ireland was back to one of the major negative benchmarks from where it started in the 1950's. Or even further back if you take into account the 85 billion euro rescue package.

The Economist noted that "sensible policies" had allowed Ireland to close the gap on other European economies. Sense seemed to have dissipated as success went to Irish politicians' heads and in 2006 Taoiseach Bertie Ahern was reported to have said that the "boom was getting boomier" and the crash came two years later.

With four other EU countries in similar circumstances and the EU itself in serious difficulties at least they can take lessons from these debacles.

Well they could ... but they didn't.

In July 2013, at the end of its six month stint as EU President, Ireland proudly unveiled the fruits of six months' work aimed towards Stability, Jobs and Growth. It was costed as follows:

70 billion* euro Horizon 2020 programme
16 billion* euro Erasmus-Plus programme
1 trillion** euro MFF

*billion = thousand million **trillion = million million

If there is anyone in the world who can understand what this means then he must be leading a very sad life.

These are incomprehensible amounts to be spent on unfathomable projects that will only sink Europe deeper into the abyss and most important, each cent of all those gazillions of euros has to come from Other Peoples' Money. This means higher taxes which in turn means less enterprise so where are jobs going to come from?

One can accuse the EU of many things but having a laugh wasn't one of them until September 2014 when the Polish Finance Minister called for 700 billion euros as an EU investment fund. This was closely followed by EU Commission President Jean-Claude Juncker's promise to set up another 300 billion euro investment package. So that's another huge financial burden for those who have to pay but to the masterminds in Brussels it is only small change.

In June 2012 Manuel Barroso, the then European Commission President, attended a G20 leaders' summit in Mexico. When asked by a Canadian journalist why North Americans should risk their assets to help Europe, Mr. Barroso angrily responded that *"we are not coming here to receive lessons …"* Without waiting for someone to ask, 'well then, where do you go?' he went on to say, *"the European Union has a model that we may be very proud of."*

Well he's entitled to his opinion but he may find that twenty five million jobless Europeans may be more inclined to agree with that Canadian journalist.

In May 2015 David Cameron led his Conservative Party to an election victory in the U.K. and his government is committed to negotiate reforms to accommodate the UK staying in the EU. On the list were things like repatriation of powers and less red tape but this doesn't even scratch the surface of the problems.

Beneath the layer of so-called respectable EU business, there is an underworld of mammoth proportions. In February 2014, the European Commissioner for Home Affairs, Cecilia Malmstrom, announced that *"corruption costs Europe 120 billion euros a year."*

To get a perspective, the European Commission's EU budget for 2012 was EUR 129. 1 billion euros so there is a parallel underworld economy in Europe with a level of funding equivalent to the annual EU budget.

In July 2014, the *New York Times* reported that all twenty-eight EU countries were being instructed to include transactions in prostitution, drugs, smuggling and any other quantifiable illicit business activities in their country's gross domestic product (GDP).

The motive is to inflate GDP figures to put a more positive gloss on debt ratios and growth figures. Some of the sordid benefits arising from this depraved thinking is to make the country's politicians look good and afford more borrowing leeway. The UK was mentioned as having fallen into line and to have taken 2009 as the starting point for compiling statistics on the benefits of these questionable activities to its economy. Who says the British are not good Europeans?

The structure of the EU is profligate above the line and dubious below so what is there to negotiate?

In 1936 Adolph Hitler marched his troops into the Rhineland in direct contravention of the Treaty of Versailles. He said he had no other territorial demands. In 1938 after he marched into Austria he said to Goebbels that Czechoslovakia was next. Hitler told Neville Chamberlain the British Prime Minister that Sudetenland would end his expansion ambitions. Neville Chamberlain wanted to help Hitler with his plans for an enlarged homeland to avoid getting Britain into conflict with Germany. In return Hitler undertook to work for the peace of Europe, Neville Chamberlain persuaded Czechoslovakia to hand over the region of Sudetenland to Hitler and came back to the UK in September 1938 waving a piece of paper declaring "peace in our time." A year later Hitler invaded Poland and Britain had to face the difficult decision it had been avoiding, namely to stand up for itself.

In May 2015 the UK prepared to negotiate the terms of its EU membership and vowed to be firm and resolute in seeking to repatriate powers ahead of the referendum. In June 2015 it was admitted that treaty changes would be unlikely before the referendum date but an irreversible and legally binding EU guarantee would be acceptable. If so Britain will have to vote on not so firm and resolute European promises which in the past British Prime Ministers had put so much faith in but were so badly let down. The vote therefore would be about whether Europe's promises are to be be trusted on this occasion. To address this concern would mean conflict with Germany so when Mr. Cameron stands in front of the British people waving his piece of paper this issue will still be smouldering. But ultimately Britain will have to face the difficult decision it had been avoiding, namely to stand up for itself.

In both cases Germany is at the heart of matters, the first time to do bad and now to do good. However in Germany's mistaken belief that it can make Europe good it is underpinning all that is bad.

Without Germany, the puffed up Eurocrats would be small time politicians limited to strutting around their own countries answerable to their own people, but Germany's obsession with a European superstate has made elephants out of mice.

As before Britain is involved but being careful not to make the waves that might rock Germany's boat.

On 27th May 2015 just prior to a tour of European capitals to press his case for EU reforms, Mr. Cameron hosted the President of the European Commission Mr. Jean-Claude Juncker who was accompanied by an expert on EU Freedom of Movement Rules which *"are central to Mr. Cameron's renegotiation demands"*.

It was also reported that they dined on Pork Belly, Spring Salad and Lime Bavarois.

"Why we will never escape from the EU" is the title of an article in the Mail on Sunday (June 2015) by Peter Hitchens. He doesn't thinks the "NO" vote will prevail in the UK referendum but even if it does *"... my own guess is that a "No" majority would not lead to a British departure from the EU ..."*

Mr. Hitchens suspects that unless the majority was so huge that it was embarrassing there will be further negotiations and more reforms and another vote in which *"you'd jolly well better vote 'Yes."*

Although not mentioned in this article, Peter Hitchens had extensively reported on a similar *"you'd jolly well better vote 'Yes'"* situation six years earlier. In June 2008 Ireland had voted "No" to the Lisbon Treaty and sixteen months later the country was hauled back for another referendum and this time the vote was "Yes".

Peter Hitchens was in Dublin to report on the immediate aftermath and surmised that the "No" vote over a year previously was the real opinion of the Irish people *"who had never liked being pushed around by outsiders"* but *"Ireland's current generation of leaders wanted a fight."*

And with good reason because according to Mr. Hitchens *"the Irish politician class sprawls luxuriously on great cushions of Euro-money ..."*

The article was entitled *"So our 1,000 years of history ends like this"* (mailonline October 2009) referring to the demise of the UK as Europe's *"oldest continuously independent sovereign state"* which indeed did come to an abrupt end with the Lisbon Treaty.

According to Open Europe the treaty caused the UK to lose its veto in one hundred and thirteen areas which meant it was now powerless to prevent legislation in those areas becoming law in Great Britain.

If the original Irish vote had stood none of this could have happened. This was contrary to the will of the politicians so the order of the day was to "frighten the shite" out of the Irish electorate to get it to reverse its decision which is what Mr. Hitchens thinks may happen in the UK if it votes NO.

What motivates politicians to revert to such tactics?

A Berliner showing a visitor around West Berlin in 1984 stopped his car outside Spandau Prison where the only prisoner Rudolf Hess, former deputy to Adolf Hitler had just turned ninety. There was general international sentiment that he should be released on humanitarian grounds and the visitor asked why not?

The Berliner had constantly hovered close to starvation during his boyhood post-war life and was still living in a city divided into four sectors, one of them communist East Berlin. Above all was his burning resentment that West Berlin was cut off from the rest of West Germany and he angrily retorted: *"If he lived till he was two hundred he should spend every single day here. These people lived like emperors and could have done so much good. Instead look what they did, they ruined my country."*

And now today's leaders dine on Pork Belly and Lime Bavarois and sprawl on great cushions of Euro-money. Still living like emperors ... still ruining countries.

Mr. Hitchens further wrote about slogans such as *"Vote Yes for jobs"* plastered all over Dublin and concluded that the Irish no longer believed they could govern their own economy.

With similar pre-referendum slogans abounding in the UK, the message emanating from the pro-EU lobby is quite clearly that without help from Brussels the British are incapable of running their own lives.

So vote to allow these emperors run your life for you? The generation of the parents of that Berliner was fully aware of the nature and character of those they voted for and not only did they bring suffering and hardship on themselves but look at the mess they left their children in.

During Mr. Cameron's two day tour of European capitals the only encouragement he appeared to have received for his hoped-for reforms was in Germany. On May 30th The Times reported that Chancellor Angela Merkel mentioned a *"flexible, two speed, unstandardised EU had long been a reality."* And on 5th June 2015 further quoted Mrs. Merkel as saying that *"we have always been able to pursue a Europe at different speeds."*

If two-speed comes about presumably the UK will be given the choice of total commitment, Euro and all, or accepting a lucky bag of concessions and joining the other less dedicated members in the slow lane. Both lanes will still be governed by Brussels except the Euro Plodders will not be sitting at the Top Table with the emperors and will have even less say than they do now.

In May 2015, *The Guardian* wrote that at its forthcoming annual dinner, the President of the Confederation of British

Industry (CBI) will be urging its members to stay in the EU. It further reported that on a previous occasion, its Director General stated that the EU needed to do more of what it is good at and less of what it is not good at. What sort of gobbledygook is that?

Business for Britain an organisation informing British companies on EU matters found that regulations since the Lisbon Treaty has so far burdened UK business with on-going annual costs in excess of STG 6 billion ... that's bad. But compared to the EUR 120 billion yearly level of corruption it almost seems good so would the CBI be happy with a few billion more of costs and a few billion less of corruption?

There is not even a plausible focal point to start making sense.

The new UK Business Secretary, Mr. Sajid Javid has consistently been sanguine about Britain outside the EU. In September 2013 he said that leaving the EU will offer Britain new opportunities and in September 2104 he suggested that Britain should have no fear of quitting the European Union.

In May 2015 the Chief Executive of the manufacturers' organisation EEF made a point of reminding Mr. Javid that most of the businesses "he will now be representing" wanted Britain to stay in a "reformed" Europe ... more gobbledygook. Britain is the only state challenging the status quo so the other twenty seven want to stay the same.

Then in June 2015 the EEF claimed "the UK has a productivity problem." Just try dumping the Lisbon Treaty's six billion annual costs and see how that improves the situation.

It is patently obvious that the EU is unreformable and no amount of pre-referendum flannel can disguise that.

A much simpler idea would be to address the real issue, namely that they have had over sixty years to get the EU working but still can't get it right ... enough already.

The ordinary people of Europe have been the suffering guinea pigs of this failed experiment for far too long. Years ago Dimitris Christoulas was unable to endure anymore and wrote how he envisaged one means of escape from the torment – *"if a fellow Greek were to grab a Kalashnikov I would be right behind him."*

CHAPTER 10

Lousy leaders make good countries lousy

"Tear down this wall!"

The words of US President Ronald Reagan aimed at his Russian counterpart Mikhail Gorbachev in June 1987. He was at the Brandenburg Gate, West Berlin during the Cold War.

In June 2012, Wolfgang Schauble told Der Spiegel, the German news magazine, that people thought the President was mad. Mr. Schauble who served as a government Minister both under Helmut Kohl and Angela Merkel, further said that in 1989, the US ambassador to the USSR suggested to him that the Berlin Wall would come down within three years.

It actually came down two years after President Reagan's speech but took less than six months from the conversation with the ambassador.

Fast forward 25 years from that 1989 meeting with the ambassador to an article in The Washington Post in March 2014 by Jack F. Matlock Jr. entitled:

> *"The U.S. has treated Russia like a loser since the end of the Cold War."*

Mr. Matlock writes that the Cold War ended not as a result of the collapse of the Soviet Union but agreements which were beneficial to both sides. The arms race was halted, chemical weapons banned and nuclear arms reduced following negotiations between US President George H.W. Bush and Mikhail Gorbachev.

The end of the Cold War was *"our common victory"* according to Mr. Gorbachev but *"… America won the Cold War"* declared Mr. Bush. Compared to the epic breakthroughs, this disagreement appears relatively cosmetic but ironically it was this dismissive attitude which radically changed Russia's perception of, and relations with, the United States.

According to Mr. Matlock, a major hammer blow was dealt on President Clinton's watch when NATO bombed Serbia without UN approval and moved into what were former Warsaw Pact countries. Previously, a huge proportion of the Russian population had had a favourable view of the Americans.

But why should the US care what Russia thinks? The Soviet Union had been the enemy for over fifty years and in the end America prevailed. Whichever way Mr. Gorbachev wanted to paint it, to the victor goes the spoils. Tough mais c'est la vie.

Yet Mr. Matlock paints a picture of the US as the bad boy.

This is not what we've been led to believe. Our leaders keep telling us that the Russians are the wicked bullies and that the virtuous, lionhearted West, especially the EU and USA, are gallantly trying to bring them to heel.

Who is this Matlock guy? Is he some sort of retro commie agitator trying to stir up trouble, and what evidence does he have to back up his claims?

The byline identifies him as "… *ambassador to the U.S.S.R. from 1987 to 1991.*"

Just a minute.....those dates would mean that he was the very same person who spoke to Herr Schauble all those years ago. As US ambassador, he must have had a ringside seat during the fall of the Soviet Union and cessation of the Cold War. As such, he undoubtedly speaks from a well-informed position so surely his first-hand experience counts as pretty solid evidence?

So whom are we to believe – Mr. Matlock or our intrepid leaders?

Where to start?

The Soviet cruise ship Maxim Gorky is as good a place as any.

On board this ship in Malta, December 1989, US President George Bush and Soviet leader Mikhail Gorbachev met at what became known as the Malta Summit. The Berlin Wall had just fallen and the headline news was the two leaders proclaiming that the Cold War had ended and an agreement being reached on nuclear arms reductions.

Behind the headlines, Helmut Kohl, the German Chancellor was pressing the US to publicly back the re-unification of Germany and one of the main Western concerns was how Russia would react to this. On the Russian side the big worry was the possible encroachment by the West into former Soviet territories.

Joshua R. Itzkowitz Shifrinson became Assistant Professor George Bush School of Government and Public Service at Texas A&M University in 2013. He published a comprehensive report of the Malta Summit, which examines the official versions from both the US and Soviet side.

The Report tells a Tale of Two Leaders, one whose world has collapsed around him and the other who had suddenly found himself on top of that world. Despite its reversal of fortune, Russia was still a nuclear power and had a considerable force of soldiers and conventional weaponry spread throughout Eastern Europe.

So the Summit was akin to two boxers circling the ring, jabbing and probing to find the other's weak points, but neither attempting a knockout punch. According to Mr. Schifrinson both the US and Soviet versions of the Summit broadly concur that Mr. Gorbachev urged the Americans to stop Cold War policies intended to *"isolate and weaken"* the USSR. But he went further … much further … out on a limb, in fact.

He asked Mr. Bush to cooperate with the USSR in the face of the imminent seed change that was about to engulf international politics. Still very much out on that limb, Mr. Gorbachev is reported to have told the Americans that all they had to was to be ready to *"gather the fruit."*

Mr. Bush assured Mr. Gorbachev that the Americans wanted perestroika to succeed, and as long as the USSR adopted a light touch towards Eastern Europe their support would continue. And the US seemed very anxious that Mr. Gorbachev's reforms should be in accordance with *"Western values"* … whatever that means.

Mr. Gorbachev's line appeared to be trying to veer towards the Americans, but Mr. Bush's seemed determined to maintain its distance. So the dialogue resembled two parallel lines which regrettably are never destined to meet and will end up who knows where?

So they were not boxers after all, just two elderly men in suits discussing the fate of mankind and one of them could have and should have done much better.

Twenty years later, a further Russian attempt to merge those parallel lines was also spurned, this time by George W. Bush.

Mr. Matlock writes that following the Twin Towers attack, the first foreign leader to call the US President was the Russian leader who had been elected just one year earlier. He not only offered support but also took the risk of lending his cooperation to America's invasion of Afghanistan and without being pressured, removing Russian bases from certain sensitive locations.

The name of this new Russian leader was a certain Vladimir Putin and according to Mr. Matlock, in return for helping the

US he received *"the diplomatic equivalent of swift kicks to the groin"* by way of a series of intrusions and interference into former Soviet territories.

These actions may not have been to Russia's liking, but following the fall of the Iron Curtain why should the Americans not be free to move into those territories if they wish?

Because they gave their word to Russia that they would not.

Pietro Shakarian, a prolific writer and commentator on Eastern European and Russian politics has written that the Bush administration informally promised that NATO would not expand *"one inch"* beyond East Germany. This has been echoed by numerous other influential personages both in interviews and written articles.

Because the undertaking was not put in writing it is subject to scepticism but Mr. Shifrinson claims that in international politics *"informal commitments count."* That's all very well, but how can you run the world on hearsay?

The big stumbling block was that without reliable assurances about American and NATO intentions in Eastern Europe, the Russians could have scuppered the reunification of Germany.

An addendum at the end of Mr. Shifrinson's report refers to a US National Security Council paper noting that the Soviets were well capable of using force to prevent *"unwelcome events"* as despite their problems, they still had 390,000 troops in East Germany.

They were also in a position to exploit the anxieties of a number of European countries who were very worried about the prospect of a unified Germany and having regard to their own experiences in the second World War, the Soviets themselves were no less anxious.

Mr. Matlock on washingtonblog.com (September 2014) wrote that he would have said *"yes there is"* if asked whether there was an understanding that NATO would not move to the east. It was not a legal commitment – more a gentlemen's agreement.

Funny thing International Politics – seems it's O.K. to go around making declarations of war but try to make a formal declaration of no war and you have a big problem.

There were a number of notable personalities to substantiate what was agreed and Mr. Matlock cites the British Prime Minister, the German Chancellor and the French President as back-up to this "handshake" agreement. Other major political figures and involved officials have also gone on record as confirming America's verbal no intrusion undertaking.

Markedly, Mr. Shifrinson notes that West German Foreign Minister Hans-Deitrich Genscher publicly declared that following reunification, NATO would not expand to the east. All this proved a strong enough mix for the Russians to put their trust in the Americans and they agreed not to stand in the way. Germany was reunited in 1990 and peace was imposed on Europe.

So how come twenty four years later all hell broke loose between the West and Russia over the former Soviet Union territory of Ukraine?

According to the Americans and the European Union it was all Russia's fault. A thundering editorial in The Times (U.K.) in February 2015 accuses Vladimir Putin of breaking deals and not abiding by the rules of "peaceful international statecraft." It was entitled "No More Appeasement."

However these views are tenable only if you set the starting point at Russia's intervention in Ukraine and do not take into account Western actions between 1990 and 2014.

Such actions listed by former US Ambassador Matlock include –

Expansion of NATO in the Balkans and Baltic
Plans for American bases there
Withdrawal from the Anti-Ballistic Missile Treaty
Invasion of Iraq without UN Security Council approval
Overt participation in the colour revolutions in Ukraine,
    Georgia and Kyrgystan
Talks with Georgia and Ukraine about joining NATO

Most of this occurred a good decade before Russia hit the headlines in connection with Ukraine. These moves certainly do not appear to embody either the letter or spirit of the US/Soviet "quid pro quo" that in return for NATO not moving into former Soviet territories, Russia would not oppose the unification of Germany.

So who's the naughty boy then?

Maybe the Russian equivalent of The Thunderer was bashing out editorials and articles demanding "No More Appeasement" following all those Western encroachments until finally the prospect of NATO forces right on their border became the last straw? Their only other option, withdrawal of support for German unification had become somewhat obsolete by then.

So "Western values" seem to be "Western" as portrayed in Wild West movies. You know, the Big Chiefs in Washington made peace treaties which were invariably broken as soon as the Indians had disarmed. With the rallying cry *"thar's gold in them thar hills"* flocks of carpetbaggers were able to flood into the territories and take as much as they could knowing that the then defenseless natives were not in much of a position to stop them.

But the Russians had more than bows and arrows to rely on and were well capable of retaliation when the West started *"… probing some of the firmest red lines any Russian leader would draw"* as Mr. Matlock described it.

Subsequent Russian conduct was considered unacceptable and on 6th March 2014 the US President signed an Executive Order which introduced sanctions against Russia for its actions against Ukraine. Europe gave its wholehearted support so the US was able to mention in its statement that the sanctions were being imposed in close coordination with the EU and other international partners.

What a jolly adventure it must have seemed to the European leaders, to be able to take on the nasty Russians with absolutely no risk to themselves as they were riding on the coattails of the mighty USA. This opportunity to clearly demonstrate that being in the EU gives member countries a much more powerful voice in the world than being independent was too good to miss.

But as soon as Russia retaliated by banning food imports from those countries which had imposed sanctions, the EU part of the international partnership started to unravel. Finland, a next door neighbour to Russia had its lorries stopped at the border causing serious economic problems especially to smaller firms and subcontractors.

Rabobank Group, a major lender to the agricultural sector in Holland reported that *"dozens of its clients"* were suffering from the shortfall in their earnings. Fruit from Poland, Spain and Belgium, cheese from France, Holland and Finland, Pork from Germany, France and Denmark were all among the products that used to flow from Europe into Russia but because of the Western sanctions had now come to an abrupt halt.

Economists rationalised that the amount of euros lost in curtailed sales to Russia compared to the overall amount of EU trade was not really that important. This ignored the fact that each statistic represented a business in trouble, a family deprived of income and livelihoods lost which to the unfortunate victims was of vital importance.

A typical example from Finland of the overnight demise of a family owned transport firm whose fleet of twelve vehicles and eighteen drivers was rendered redundant was mirrored all over Europe.

"Like shooting oneself in the foot," commented the Hungarian Prime Minister but as usual it was the citizens who were injured and not one report came through of a politician who was limping as the result of a gunshot wound.

Certainly the Russians were hurt by the sanctions, they admitted it themselves, but Europe was seriously damaged also, not only by the Russian retaliation but also by their own self-imposed ban on selling certain products to Russia. Such as France stopping delivery of a Mistral naval helicopter carrier at the cost of a billion euros plus millions more in penalty charges. And the delivery of a second ship the following year was also put in doubt.

A French trade union official said that the shipyard workers were "outraged" at the French government's actions. They may also have been outraged at Russia's actions in Ukraine but if they were, then obviously not to the extent of losing their jobs.

It transpired that others where jobs had disappeared or were at risk, felt the same and expressed as much by ditching the communal approach and taking an independent line. Those included an influential Irish agricultural organisation which urged Ireland to turn its back on European bloc discussions and *"promote its own interest with the Russian authorities."*

The Cypriot President on a visit to Moscow was offered continuing help and support by Mr. Putin over his country's debt crisis. Mr. Anastasiades told reporters that EU sanctions were a source of wider problems for the whole EU and for good measure threw in the announcement that the Russian Navy would be allowed to use Cypriot ports.

Prior to his visit to Mr. Putin in April 2015, the Greek Prime Minister, in an interview with Tass the Russian news service, described the sanctions as "senseless" and informed the EU that it should not take for granted Greece's ongoing support for them. After his meeting with Mr. Putin, Mr. Tsipras came away with the offer of a trade deal which apparently was also on the table for any EU member which countered the sanction programme.

If anyone was wondering what life will be like when the European Union becomes a Federal Superstate, this could be described as a full dress rehearsal. The one sure thing to be learned from this affair is that when it really is show time, it is definitely not going to be alright on the night.

The cast of individual nations had clearly shown that it is unable to shed the grassroots affinity to its own respective traditions and cultures. These characteristics have always been the innate tools of survival and continuity of any country, large or small, and when Greece and Cyprus found themselves being crushed and suffocated by the steamroller policies of their bigger partners, they reached out to whatever levers they could grasp that might open channels to allow them to breathe again.

As events showed, they were well capable of striding the world stage as solo artists without having to be just another lowly extra in the twenty eight strong EU Chorus line to garner an audience. This is contrary to what the leaders of much bigger countries believe is possible for themselves and try to have us believe also.

In February 2015 a report from Caritas Europa revealed that in Bulgaria, Greece, Latvia and Hungary over a third of the population was teetering on the edge of poverty and in fourteen of the EU's twenty eight member states at least a third of the children were already living in poverty. The growing evidence is ominous. It points more and more to the likelihood that Greece is actually a microcosm of how many other countries around Europe are going to end up under EU restrictions and rules.

Paul Krugman writing in The New York Times expressed amazement how those in the European Commission could be so confident about what to do in the current crisis when in previous crises they had been wrong about everything.

Not only have things significantly deteriorated since that was written in March 2013 but then they took it upon themselves to go way beyond their own borders to pick a fight with Russia which only exacerbated an already disastrous situation.

Similar situations in the not so distant past were handled in a far more practical and less harmful manner and the actions of the governments of that time make a sobering comparison with the policies of today's administrators.

As a backdrop, in the early 1960's Dr. David Thornley, Professor of Political Science in Trinity College Dublin, addressing his class said *"this week we are going to study the free press in the Western World."* The following week he told his class *"this week we are going to study the free press in the Soviet Union."*

This was around the period of the Cuban Missile Crisis and there was uproar in the class. When the furore had died down, Dr. Thornley calmly explained that the Soviet Union also claimed to have a free press and they were going to spend the week studying it.

In those days, universities considered it essential to give a comprehensive and balanced training to their students. It is known as seeing the other guy's point of view and enabled the student in later life to make even-handed assessments when confronted with various problems and dilemmas.

By way of illustration, a foreign student on an international work exchange programme in Helsinki, Finland in 1964 happened to pass a field filled with motor bikes on his way to work each day. He asked his boss and was told that they were Russian motor bikes. "O.K. *but why are they just lying in a field?*" asked the student. *"Because nobody wants them"* said his boss. *"Then why are the bikes there in the first place?"* the student persisted. *"Because if we don't buy their motor bikes, the Russians won't buy our dairy products"* came the reply.

This was really bad Cold War time when there were almost daily reports of people being shot trying to escape East Berlin. The Finns presumably found this abhorrent, but in those days they made their own choices on how to live their lives so they chose to establish a modus vivendi with their neighbour and sell their dairy products even if it meant filling fields with motorbikes that nobody wanted.

Half a century later Finland was suddenly unable to sell its dairy products to its neighbour Russia and the President of Finland is reported to have expressed "great concern" which is probably as robust a response he felt he could utter without causing offence to his EU partners. This is hardly in the same league as the principled stand his fellow countrymen took in 1939 when they as good as told Joseph Stalin to "piss off" in response to the territorial adjustments he proposed to them in the full knowledge that their refusal to co-operate would inevitably lead to war between Finland and Russia.

Throughout the Iron Curtain and Berlin Wall era, politicians generally made an effort to go that extra mile to try to see the other guy's point of view. Despite intermittent flare ups, this attitude resulted in nations with completely contrasting philosophies still being able to trade and interact with each other. It used to be called co-existence. The alternative was considered too perilous.

Just over fifty years have passed and things are so different. As it continued to expand, co-existence gradually succumbed to the EU doctrine of "my way or the highway." This is based on policies formed from the perspective of EU tunnel vision and is dismissive of any other viewpoint. The Russian sanctions is a glaring example of how ethically ruinous this can be.

Turkey invaded Cyprus in July 1974 and today still holds 36% of the geographical territory of the island. Sanctions were imposed on products from the now "Turkish Republic of Northern Cyprus" but surprisingly not on Turkey, the actual invader. When Cyprus became a member of the European Union in May 2004 it automatically meant that a foreign invader was (and still is) occupying a part of EU territory. And there's more …

In October 2014 when oil exploration off Cyprus looked optimistic, a Turkish survey vessel located itself within Cypriot territorial waters to observe the exploratory deep-sea drilling. The EU/US reaction was as follows – the US Ambassador to Cyprus said on CyBC TV that Turkey's actions were a violation of international law and the European Council expressed serious concern and urged Turkey to show restraint and respect Cyprus sovereignty.*

(*Turkey does not officially recognise the sovereignty of the Republic of Cyprus so fat lot of use that must have been)

Enter the Russian/Ukraine problem and suddenly screams of righteous indignation and calls for vigorous action. Equivalence would have been to limit sanctions to the rebel held areas of Ukraine but Russia does not want to become a member of the EU whereas Turkey commenced discussions to join in 2005 ... so lack of equivalence is not so surprising after all.

Two questions, firstly if over twenty years of sanctions haven't worked in tiny Northern Cyprus what rationale was there to believe they would work against formidable Russia? Secondly how is it justifiable to commit to a cause outside EU jurisdiction and ignore a similar situation which has been festering in its own back yard for over ten years? Although Cyprus may be a relatively small island the impact of the invasion was huge with 200,000 Greek Cypriots having been forced to leave their homes.

The European Court of Human Rights in more than twenty judgements favoured former Greek Cypriot house owners dispossessed by the invasion. The compensation awarded was significant. A 2003 award in the case of Demades vs Turkey was EUR 750,000. The Court also ruled that Greek Cypriots in general could not be deemed to have lost title to their property and the awards were for losses from not being able to access their properties.

To date, only one case has been paid and Turkey doesn't seem very perturbed, unlike U.K. politicians who tremble in fear of EU repercussions should British farmers grow a cauliflower just one millimetre outside EU regulations.

Even in the face of a multitude of judicial rulings against Turkey, EU leaders chose to ignore the glaring outrage within their own borders and instead set off on a Don Quixote* type foray miles away from home. However the results of their domestic campaigns do not inspire much confidence that they will fare any better abroad.

*Don Quixote is the comic hero of Spanish novelist Miguel de Cervantes (1547–1616) who journeys around Spain seeking to right wrongs in the name of chivalry. He invariably ends up getting bashed because of completely misjudging situations and his sidekick Sancho Panza is the recipient of multiple thumpings simply because he is with him.

The EU is supposed to act in accordance with its bible "A Constitution for Europe" and one of its main objectives is *"the combating of social exclusion."* This is the intent, but the actuality is the very opposite. Social exclusion exists on a spectacular scale because of its failure to accomplish an even more fundamental objective, *"aiming at full employment."* Around twenty-five million unemployed is a fair indication of how bad its aim is.

In the section "Common Foreign and Security Policy", Member States must support the foreign policy *"actively and unreservedly in a spirit of loyalty and mutual solidarity."*

Chapter 2, Paragraph 2 clearly says that they (member states) *"shall refrain from any action which is … likely to impair its effectiveness as a cohesive force in international relations"* and *"the Council and the Union Minister for Foreign Affairs shall ensure these principles are complied with."*

SOURCE: TREATY ESTABLISHING A CONSTITUTION FOR EUROPE – LUXEMBOURG: OFFICE FOR OFFICIAL PUBLICATIONS OF THE EUROPEAN COMMUNITIES 2005

By July 2014, less than six months after the imposition of the sanctions against Russia which is obviously "foreign policy", at least nine EU countries were identified as openly opposed to and prepared to block the sanctions. This is blatantly contrary to *"a spirit of loyalty and mutual solidarity"* and nearly a third of the Member States opting out is surely *"likely to impair the EU's effectiveness as a cohesive force in international relations."*

These are clear breaches so the Council and the Union Minister for Foreign Affairs, as directed by their Constitution, must ensure that the *"principles are complied with."* By the next sanction vote all the dissenters had fallen back into line but apparently it wasn't all due to EU diligence.

A press release from the US Embassy in Athens said that the Assistant Secretary of State for European and Eurasian Affairs had visited Athens in March and discussed the crisis in Ukraine among other issues. Local commentator's filling in more detail called it an ultimatum against breaking ranks with the NATO allies against Russia. They further reported that the Assistant Secretary also warned Mr. Tsipras not to default on its debts to Germany, the ECB and IMF.

The damage from losing trade with Russia caused those nine EU countries to openly oppose the sanctions in the first place. This had not changed by the time it came to the vote so one wonders what pressures had been applied to get them to vote in favour of continued damage to their countries?

Mr. Tsipras did not create the circumstances nor the system which brought the austerity measures but seeing the harm it was doing he dared to go against its rules to try to alleviate the suffering in his country. He was accused of being misguided and deluded and was scorned by the western press and politicians who accused him of being naive and unrealistic because he didn't understand that the Euro system did not allow for such accommodations and his proposals could lead to its break up.

In 1968 Alexander Dubcek leader of Czechoslovakia introduced reforms leading to new freedoms for the Czechs. The Soviet system did not allow for such accommodations and

Moscow feared it would lead to the break-up of the Warsaw Pact so it invaded the country and put an end to the Dubcek reforms. Mr. Dubcek was brought to Moscow and pressures behind closed doors forced him to publicly recant when he returned to Czechoslovakia.

What's the difference? Mr. Dubcek had dared to go against the rules of the Soviet system to try to improve conditions in the lives of the Czech people and the western press and politicians cheered him on and hailed him as a hero and were up in arms when the Soviets put an end to his campaign.

It clearly shows that any project that puts doctrinaire policies before people can only survive if it reverts to methods resembling those that were previously used to maintain the Soviet system. No explanation was forthcoming as to how come those EU states which had openly opposed the sanctions because of the economic damage to their economies, voted to continue harming their own countries when it came to the crunch.

Surely the citizens of those countries should be demanding an explanation of their representatives as to whom and what they are actually representing?

Greece is flayed for defying the conditions imposed on it but as the EU itself flouts the provisions of its own Constitution it is surely in no position to preach. Not content with the havoc they have caused within their own jurisdiction the European leaders have now turned their attention to matters outside.

"They understand very little," said Helmut Schmidt former German Chancellor referring to EU Commissioners' interference in Ukraine. *"This is megalomania – we have no business being there."*

Peter Hitchens writing in the Mail on Sunday (March 2104) wrote *"Stupidity and ignorance rule the world. Trouble is that the stupid and ignorant think they are clever and well-informed."* He states that we are being dragged into a new Cold War by *"… silly, half educated politicians of today* (who) … *still like to pose as tough guys."*

These comments may sound somewhat over the top but it was the politicians themselves who set out "the founding principles of the Union", the attainment of which was way beyond their capabilities. They are punching well above their weight and the Constitution is a perfect case in point.

A written constitution is a "sacred" implement by which a country or organisation can be run and those who choose to have one must observe its provisions to the letter. If not the citizens, members or shareholders can make the administrators legally accountable so in that context "A Constitution for Europe" is not a constitution. More appropriately it should be renamed "A Wish List for Europe" and like most wish lists should be acknowledged as being in the realms of fantasyland.

In April 2015 at yet another crisis meeting about the latest crises in the saga of the Greek crisis The Times reported that EU finance ministers *"have spent their entire tenures dealing not with their own country's affairs but with Greece's problems.*

Why were those finance ministers not at home carrying out their duties to their own people? They tell us they were dealing with Greece's problems but is that the real reason?

For an answer one needs to go to Frankfurt, Germany when in May 2010 the ground-breaking ceremony for the new premises of the European Central Bank (ECB) took place. Originally the cost was not to exceed 500 million euros but when it was inaugurated some five years later in March 2015 the cost had risen to 1.15 billion euros with a final estimate of a possible 1.3 billion euros.

During the time of construction, the ECB as part of the

Troika had kept Greece in a financial straightjacket. The Greek opposition Syriza party came to power at the end of 2014 and in March 2015 it undertook to provide food stamps and free electricity to Greece's poorest households and abolish a compulsory 5-euro fee for hospital visits. Humanitarian as this may have been the European Union opposed such moves and was forthright in its displeasure.

Isn't that pretty rich coming from people who were responsible for a potential overspend of one hundred and seventy million euros for each year it took to build a new home for their representatives to the Troika? What are their qualifications to give lectures on belt tightening?

Sure Greece got itself into trouble but the medicine was wrong because those prescribing it did not have the patient's best interests in mind. The Euro was the prime consideration and let the devil take the patient.

Mr. Yanis Varoufakis on German TV before he became Finance Minister, said that Greece will never pay its debts and the EU had known this in 2010. He further called it a crime against humanity to give *"the most bankrupt of all countries the largest credit in history"* because it pushed Greece into permanent debt. The amount of the bailout then was a cool two hundred and forty billion euros so despite the rhetoric Mr. Varfoufakis's assessment seems perfectly reasonable.

Like any individual or corporation overwhelmed by debt, the more appropriate course of action would have been a default or a workable arrangement with its creditors.

But that's not the way things work in the EU because it would have jeopardised the Euro and embarrassed the almighty ECB which controls the economies of the nineteen Eurozone countries ... yet was unable to calculate the correct cost of its shiny new 45-storey skyscraper.

Back to the finance ministers and why they were never at home. Their job was not to help Greece but to preserve the Euro at any cost, or at least make sure that it stays in until a smooth exit could be arranged – smooth for the EU that is. In any clash between an institution and the people, the institution will always win irrespective of the human cost.

This became crystal clear when photos of a Greek pensioner crying on the pavement because he wasn't able to withdraw his pension after trying four different banks, went around the world. He was recognised by a business man in Australia who offered support and organised a charitable collection because he would not allow *"a proud hardworking man to starve"*. Sir Stelios Haji-Ioannou, founder of the airline EasyJet provides around 2,500 snacks every day in Athens and soon this may rise to 3,000. *"A sandwich or croissant may not sound a lot but for some people it's vital"* he said.

While squeezing the life out of Greece to repay an unre-payable loan there was the further obscenity of the European Central Bank then into its seventh of a twenty one month quan-titive easing programme consisting of pumping sixty billion euros each month into the Euro area.

Despite all those hundreds of billions of euros of extra liquidity sloshing around Europe Australians still felt obliged to send charity from the other side of the world to prevent EU citizens from going hungry.

When Bernard Connolly wrote "The Rotten Heart of Europe" which was highly critical of the proposed Euro, the year was 1995. At that time there were no overt signs of the rot but by 2015 it can be seen to have infested the whole continent.

In the U.K., scaremongering headlines, mostly from Establishment and political leaders abound like *"City big hitters warn of disaster on EU exit"*, *"Millions of jobs at risk if we leave the EU", "We must stay in Europe, says CBI"* and *"Labour: We'll forge closer links with EU."*

Change is anathema to the Establishment because it always reckons it is better off staying rooted to the spot – that's why it is called Establishment. Now that the body of Europe has been shown to be riddled with the rot that Bernard Connolly first discovered in its heart twenty years ago, what they took to be solid ground has turned out to be a very slippery slope.

The writing has been on the wall for quite some time and whether the UK stays in or leaves will prove to be of little relevance to the inevitable outcome. Those interested in their own survival would be well advised to pay heed to the words of Charles Darwin who said that it was not the strongest nor most intelligent that survive, but *"the one most responsive to change"*.

Regrettably history has shown that change was never on the agenda of the European Establishment and always had to be imposed by either invading armies or internal rebellion so it may have been no exaggeration when Dimitris Christoulas wrote *"young people with no future will one day take up arms and hang the traitors … just like the Italians did to Mussolini in 1945"*

CHAPTER 10½

All the world's a stage
and
Europe is the pantomime district

ACT 1

***

SCENE: Headquarters of CONTINENTAL FEDERAL ENTERPRISE LTD.
Chairman is showing around a group of important investors

CHAIRMAN: *This office is our main planning centre.*

PENSION FUND MANAGER: *Wow! It's huge … it's palatial.*

CHAIRMAN: *All our premises are just as lavish and as you can see the staff are hard at work.*

PENSION FUND MANAGER: *Indeed, they look very busy but there are so many of them. What exactly do they do?*

CHAIRMAN: *They are devising rules and regulations to make it more complicated and costly for us to do business.*

PENSION FUND MANAGER: *What? Are you saying that all these people are paid to come up with ideas for obstacles to make life difficult for your other divisions?*

CHAIRMAN: *Absolutely, and they're doing a great job. We've had little or no growth for the past few years and we've been able to make loads of people unemployed.*

STOCKBROKER: *But why would you want to deliberately handicap perfectly good businesses?*

CHAIRMAN: *As you are aware, the wealth gap has become an uncomfortable issue so by handicapping those who are doing well we are able to narrow this divide.*

STOCKBROKER: *But that just makes the good not so good. It won't make the not so good any better. All you achieve is universally low standards.*

CHAIRMAN: *We prefer to call it a level playing field.*

STOCKBROKER: *How does this all work out financially?*

CHAIRMAN: *See for yourself – here are our latest accounts.*

HE HANDS OUT COPIES. THEY READ.

STOCKBROKER: *Look here … your auditors have refused to sign them off.*

CHAIRMAN: *Oh, that's normal.*

STOCKBROKER: *Why's that?*

CHAIRMAN: *We can't figure it out.*

STOCKBROKER: *According to the notes, there's not enough detail about where the money goes.*

CHAIRMAN: *They're always like that, but we just give it out. What do they want from us? Anyway, there's always more money coming in, so where's the problem? Let's move on – these are the offices for our Directors and we recruit their assistants from universities all over.*

INSURANCE EXECUTIVE: *Presumably you get the high achievers?*

CHAIRMAN: *No way! We specifically target those who can't get jobs in their own countries.*

EXECUTIVE: *Why's that?*

CHAIRMAN: *Our directors were not very good in their home offices – that's why they were sent here in the first place. The last thing we need is over-qualified subordinates showing them up.*

EXECUTIVE: *How on earth can this be of benefit to your company?*

CHAIRMAN: *Isn't it obvious? By keeping standards so low, any Tom, Dick or Harry can join and now we're the biggest in the world.*

EXECUTIVE: *Biggest what?*

CHAIRMAN: *Exactly*

COMPANY DIRECTOR: *Want to know something? If you were making products you'd have gone bust long ago.*

CHAIRMAN: *But we do make things.*

COMPANY DIRECTOR: *I don't believe it – what?*

CHAIRMAN: *We concoct devices to create employment.*

COMPANY DIRECTOR: *Are they any good?*

CHAIRMAN: *Yes and no.*

COMPANY DIRECTOR: *What's the "yes" and what's the "no"?*

CHAIRMAN: *Yes, there's lots of people employed making up the devices but no they don't create employment when they're released. In fact the very opposite – they create massive unemployment.*

COMPANY DIRECTOR: *So what do you do?*

CHAIRMAN: *We keep trying to get them working.*

COMPANY DIRECTOR: *How?*

CHAIRMAN: *By throwing more money at them.*

COMPANY DIRECTOR: *And will you ever be able to get them up and running?*

CHAIRMAN: *Not a hope.*

COMPANY DIRECTOR: *So how do you keep getting the money?*

CHAIRMAN: *From the shareholders of course.*

COMPANY DIRECTOR: *But why do they keep investing in things that will never work?*

CHAIRMAN: *They believe what we tell them.*

COMPANY DIRECTOR: *Then your directors must be absolutely stupid for wasting so much money.*

CHAIRMAN: *It's not the directors who are stupid.*

COMPANY DIRECTOR: *How's that?*

CHAIRMAN: *Because it's not their own money that they're wasting.*

COMPANY DIRECTOR: *How do they get away with it?*

CHAIRMAN: *We train them how to fool the public.*

COMPANY DIRECTOR: *So you tell them what to say?*

CHAIRMAN: *Oh no, they already know what to say. The very fact they are here is proof of that. We just coach them in the finer, more subtle points so they come across "life and death" convincing.*

COMPANY DIRECTOR: *What does that mean?*

CHAIRMAN: *As you well know, we can't point to successes so our representatives have to revert to scaremongering like telling the public that if they think the past was bad, the future will be even worse if they don't keep supporting us.*

COMPANY DIRECTOR: *So what's the secret for getting this misleading message across?*

CHAIRMAN: *Wear an expensive suit.*

COMPANY DIRECTOR: *And that's it?*

CHAIRMAN: *Well, a good shirt and tie can't hurt.*

COMPANY DIRECTOR: *That's not what I mean – it's just that what you're saying sounds very far-fetched.*

CHAIRMAN: *But it always works. Whenever we have a catastrophe, it's a proven fact that we have been able to convince people that it's in their best interest. Do you honestly think they would swallow that from someone wearing jeans and a T shirt?*

COMPANY DIRECTOR: *O.K. but when results ultimately tell a different story, won't the game be up?*

CHAIRMAN: *It's much too late by then. That official will have moved on and a new one in his place.*

COMPANY DIRECTOR: *Wearing an expensive suit, no doubt.*

CHAIRMAN: *Now you've got it!*

THEY WALK ON

HEDGE FUND MANAGER: *My goodness, look – so many containers over there. What's going on?*

CHAIRMAN: *That's the despatch area for our exports.*

HEDGE FUND MANAGER: PUTTING HAND TO HIS NOSE *That disgusting stench … is it coming from that giant rubbish dump?*

CHAIRMAN: *That dump is all the apples, meat and food that should have gone to Russia.*

HEDGE FUND MANAGER: *That's a huge amount of waste. It must cost a lot of money to have to dump it all.*

CHAIRMAN: *Not really, probably around a few billion Ajokes.*

HEDGE FUND MANAGER: *A few billion what?*

CHAIRMAN: *Ajokes. That's our currency.*

HEDGE FUND MANAGER: *You have your own currency?*

CHAIRMAN: *Why not? America is Dollar. Britain is Sterling. Ours is Ajoke.*

HEDGE FUND MANAGER: *Did the Russians actually cancel their order?*

CHAIRMAN: *In a manner of speaking. They refused to take our food products because we stopped our banks from dealing with them. Also we stopped supplying them with capital equipment and technical support.*

HEDGE FUND MANAGER: *Why would you do that?*

CHAIRMAN: *Because we don't like the morality of Russia's leaders.*

HEDGE FUND MANAGER *But you can't do business on the basis of some vague measurement of a customers' so-called morality and anyway there are many much worse.*

CHAIRMAN: *Maybe, but the Russians keep trying to prevent their neighbours from joining us.*

HEDGE FUND MANAGER: *But how can you justify not trading with them on that sort of a basis? What sort of ethic is that?*

CHAIRMAN: *We like to use the term Creating Responses as Appropriate by Proxy. This is an innovation we developed in-house so nowadays when we have to explain things we don't understand we find that reverting to CRAP proves very effective.*

HEDGE FUND MANAGER: *And I thought you were a Trade Organisation.*

CHAIRMAN: *That's the general idea, but we appear to spend so much time tied up in other peoples' affairs that we never seem to be able to get around to trading.*

THEY WALK ON

NEWSPAPER EDITOR: *Those people we just passed, what language are they speaking?*

CHAIRMAN: *I have no idea, but that's not unusual. Very few people in our organisation are able to understand one another.*

NEWSPAPER EDITOR: *But why would you employ people who can't communicate with each other?*

CHAIRMAN: *We have to. Free movement of labour and all that …*

NEWSPAPER EDITOR: *They're loading all those crates on to such a long line of lorries. That must be a gigantic export order.*

CHAIRMAN: *Actually those crates are full of our own stuff.*

NEWSPAPER EDITOR: *What sort of stuff?*

CHAIRMAN: *Our files and records. We can't operate without those.*

NEWSPAPER EDITOR: *Are you moving?*

CHAIRMAN: *Yes. Four hundred and thirty kilometres away.*

NEWSPAPER EDITOR: *And these offices are being sold?*

CHAIRMAN: *Heavens no. We only spend four days in the other offices and then we come back here.*

NEWSPAPER EDITOR: *Just a minute. Are you telling us that you pack everything away, travel four hundred and thirty kilometres with your staff, go to all the trouble of unpacking and setting up, pack up again and then come back here … leaving these perfectly good offices empty for four days? How mad is that?*

CHAIRMAN: *It's not so mad. The other offices, which are just as good, are left empty for much longer.*

NEWSPAPER EDITOR: *And I suppose you're going to tell us that you do this every other week?*

CHAIRMAN: *Don't be ridiculous, we're not fools. We only do it once a month!*

CURTAIN

ACT 2

SCENE: Meeting of Main Board of Directors

UK: *Thank you so much for taking the time to have this meeting. I know how very busy you are …*

GERMANY: (interrupting) *Oh just get on with what you have to say.*

UK. *We would be ever so grateful if you could make some reforms so we can show that being part of your organisation is really good for us.*

GERMANY: *What reforms?*

UK: *We are being swamped with newcomers and can't afford to absorb even those who are already here, let alone having to take in more. It is essential that we get back the powers to control the numbers coming into our area.*

GERMANY: *Out of the question! There has to be free movement of people and as long as the cleverest and hardest working keep coming to us, that's the way it will stay. Anything else?*

UK: *Our financial division has been severely weakened since you imposed pay level rules. We need to be able to remunerate as we see fit. After all, we are in a free market economy.*

GERMANY: *You gave that up when you signed with us.*

UK: *But if newcomers are free how come money isn't?*

GERMANY: *Your financial centre by far outperforms the others and our mission is all about sharing success with those who are less capable.*

UK: *But the others are rubbish.*

GERMANY: *That's the sort of talk one expects from someone acting independently. You now have partners so you must be prepared to share what you have with those less capable.*

UK: *Let me make it clear, we are honoured to be part of this great venture but in continually giving so much to so many of what we regard as "shitty little operators", we have become one ourselves.*

GERMANY: *And is that not proof of our success? Instead of twenty eight independent units all competing against each other, with our guidance we have managed to get twenty seven of them operating on the same level with none of them able to compete with anyone. You should be proud but instead all you do is complain.*

UK: *With respect, you are not equal with the others.*

GERMANY: *Someone has to conduct the orchestra and that's not an easy task when half the musicians are never in tune and the other half haven't a clue how to play.*

UK: *Then why do you do it?*

GERMANY: *We had to bail out those who didn't follow the rules, so we don't feel guilty about bending or even breaking them ourselves. However we don't want to be accused of bringing it down altogether so we do our best. Our priority is shielding ourselves from the worst effects but if the others are prepared let themselves to go to hell, then why should we care? Now, is that it?*

UK: *Well there is something else …*

GERMANY: *What?*

UK: *We are constantly being smothered with mountains of Red Tape. To be honest, it's difficult to tell which is worse – the Red Tape or the newcomers.*

GERMANY: (losing composure) *Donner und Blitzen!! Red tape is the ketchup that keeps the burger together. Do you not understand that without the constant flow of Red Tape the public would clearly see what was going on and that would be kaput to our glorious project.*

UK: *But I'm worried that if you don't give me a few concessions I may lose support for staying in your organisation.*

GERMANY: *Mein lieber freund no one asked you to have a vote.*

UK: *And that's it?*

GERMANY: *Well there may be something we can do. We're considering splitting ourselves into two tiers and if you agreed to be relegated we could offer you the same package as the others in the lower division.*

UK: *What sort of package?*

GERMANY: *We haven't all the details yet but it would be much less stringent than for premier members so I can tell you that there will definitely be concessions for the also rans.*

UK: *Sounds great. We agree. Where do I sign?*

GERMANY: *Not so fast. We need something from you in exchange.*

UK: *Anything – what do you want?*

GERMANY: *You will be expected to put a lot of effort and resources behind your campaign to stay in.*

UK: *Does that include money?*

GERMANY: *Of course … lots.*

UK: *Is that really necessary?*

GERMANY: *Guter mann, not everybody thinks as highly of our organisation as you do so you will have to spin as you've never spun to make us look really good. Now is that all?*

UK: *Before I go please allow me to express our sincere gratitude for giving us such a strong voice in the decision making process.*

EXIT UK

GERMANY: *Gott in himmel but those Britishers are hard work. Now to serious business.* Turns to France *Have you come to any conclusions on what we discussed?*

FRANCE: *I believe we have. If you agree to turn a blind eye and avoid criticising our excessive losses for the next three years, we would be prepared to meet you half way on the duplicate HQ issue.*

GERMANY: *What exactly are you proposing?*

FRANCE: *That we put an end to the monthly four day session that we host …*

GERMANY: *Sounds promising …*

FRANCE: *… and make it just two days!!*

GERMANY: *Verdammt! Are you serious?*

FRANCE: *Is anything wrong?*

GERMANY: *Nein … nein … I suppose we could announce it at the next meeting and present it as a ground-breaking step forward and that it demonstrates to our critics that our organisation is not a complete waste of space after all.*

FRANCE: *Do you think that will work?*

GERMANY: *Ach so … it keeps getting more difficult to keep this car crash on the road, but that pathetic shower believes anything I tell them, so why not?*

FRANCE + GERMANY: *Let's do it!!*

CURTAIN

HISTORICAL FOOTNOTE

Archaeologists excavating ruins in the environs of a large city in Belgium recently discovered a plaque which reads

> *"Never in the field of human endeavour has so much been owed"*

PERMISSIONS (in alphabetical order)

Corporate Europe Observatory (CEO)
Curtis Brown Group (The Estate of Winston S. Churchill)
Encyclopaedia Britannica
eureferendum.com
Frankfurter Allgemeine Zeitung
Guardian News and Media
Daniel Hannan MEP
The Independent
Independent News & Media (Ireland)
Josef Joffe
Max Keiser
Liebnitz Institute for Economic Research at the University of
    Munich
maltatoday.com
Jack Matlock
News Syndication (*The Times*)
Robert O. Paxton
Proto Thema (Athens)
Publications Office Of The European Union
Peter Schneider
Solo Syndication (*The Mail on Sunday* and Mailonline)
The Spectator
Telegraph Media Group
World Socialist Website (wsws.org)

About the Author

Maurice Feldman was born in Dublin, Ireland on 8th August 1942 and has a brother and sister still living in Dublin.

His early education was at Rathgar National Primary School and Stratford College Secondary School, which was founded by his mother.

As a student, he used to write serious editorials and satirical articles for communal and college magazines and comedy sketches for local theatre.

He studied Economics,Commerce and French at Trinity College Dublin, and on finishing University in 1964, with BA BComm degrees, ran Metal Spinners Ltd., a factory manufacturing Aluminium and Copper Pots, Pans and Electric Kettles. The factory was in a small township called Newtownmountkennedy in Co. Wicklow, about 35 kms from Dublin.

He married Barbara in 1973 and left Metal Spinners a year later when it was taken over by a large UK public company. By then, there were about 100 workers and its products were being sold to the UK, Europe and Australia.

In 1979 Maurice and Barbara set up their own factory in Dublin, manufacturing Sachets of Sugar, Salt, Pepper and non Dairy Creamer. They also made plastic Cocktail Stirs (swizzle sticks) on a minor scale. The sachet business was sold in the late 1980's and the Cocktail Stirs were developed into their major activity, selling all over Europe and Scandinavia.

When their two sons Daniel and Jonathan graduated from UK universities they left Ireland for London in 2003, where Barbara had been establishing a packaging distribution business.

On moving to London Maurice decided to take up writing full time and opted to keep taking writing courses until something came up that he felt he could work on. He took a series of ten week writing courses in City Lit, Covent Garden - Creative Writing, Comedy Scripts and Journalism.

As a class exercise in Journalism he had written a piece called Alice in Euroland. When some months later he read of the suicide of Dimitris Christoulas in Athens he felt that the note Mr. Christoulas left behind portrayed the EU in a different and original light and decided to develop this further as a book.